Arrow Books

Citizens' Rights

General Editor: Frank Field
Director of the Child Poverty Action Group

Much legislation has been designed to give ordinary people a far
better deal. But politicians and lawyers overlooked one crucial fact.
We don't all speak or understand their language.
Unlike the official handouts, this series is written by experts whose
work is to help people understand and claim their rights. In other
words it has been written with you in mind.
Each guide can be read without referring to any other material.
They each deal with all the main issues where you, the citizen, find
that 'they' are not telling you all you ought to know.

Legal Rights
Henry Hodge

Henry Hodge works as the Child Poverty Action Group's solicitor
where he specializes in social security, housing problems and the
legal rights of low income families. He is a member of the Executive
of the National Council for Civil Liberties and is also on the
Islington Council.

Henry Hodge

Legal Rights

Arrow Books

Arrow Books Ltd
3 Fitzroy Square, London W1

London Melbourne Sydney Auckland
Wellington Johannesburg Cape Town
and agencies throughout the world

First published in Arrow Books Ltd 1974
© Henry Hodge 1974
Diagrams © Arrow Books Ltd 1974

Set in Monotype Times
Printed in Great Britain by The Anchor Press Ltd
and bound by Wm Brendon & Son Ltd, both of
Tiptree, Essex

For Miranda

ISBN 0 09 909890 3

Acknowledgements

I would like to thank Cyril Glasser, Frank Field,
Julian Gibson-Watt, Larry Grant, Stuart Weir, Anne
Winyard and Ruth Lister for their very helpful comments
and suggestions on the draft of this book

how Civil Courts referred to in the book are arranged

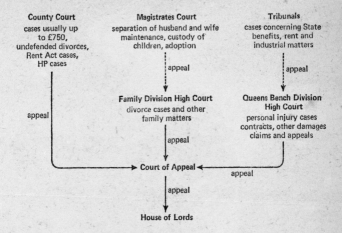

County Court
cases usually up
to £750,
undefended divorces,
Rent Act cases,
HP cases

Magistrates Court
separation of husband and wife
maintenance, custody of
children, adoption

appeal

Tribunals
cases concerning State
benefits, rent and
industrial matters

appeal

Family Division High Court
divorce cases and other
family matters

appeal

**Queens Bench Division
High Court**
personal injury cases
contracts, other damages
claims and appeals

appeal

Court of Appeal ◄

appeal

appeal

House of Lords

how Criminal Courts referred to in the book are arranged

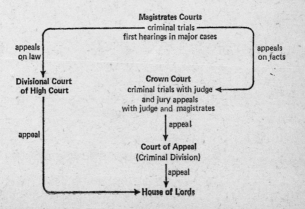

Magistrates Courts
criminal trials
first hearings in major cases

appeals
on law

appeals
on facts

**Divisional Court
of High Court**

Crown Court
criminal trials with judge
and jury appeals
with judge and magistrates

appeal

appeal

Court of Appeal
(Criminal Division)

appeal

House of Lords

Author's Note

Scotland has a different legal system and different courts to those in England and Wales and this book does not cover Scottish law.

Contents

Introduction

The role of the law

The law provides a framework for our lives. It controls our relationships with other people and allows us to do some things while restraining us from doing others. So most of our activities are affected in some way by the law.

When you walk down a street you are using your right to be on the highway. When you buy goods in a shop you create a contract which gives you and the seller various rights and obligations. Marriage creates legal obligations between husband and wife and these obligations can only be removed by using the law to get a divorce. We are usually most aware of the law when our rights are denied or our interests need protecting both now and for the future. So if you don't know your rights or how the legal system works you can be at a great disadvantage. And if you cannot get advice and help with problems then your knowledge may not be very useful. This book is designed as a brief guide to the law and legal problems.

Part I describes how to get help and advice with legal problems and how the legal system works.

Part II looks at some of the more common legal problems which people have to face.

Part One

How to get Help and Advice with Legal Problems: How the Legal System Works

1 How the Law Works

How law is made

Our legal system is based on laws made by Parliament and cases decided in courts or tribunals. Law has to be reasonably precise but it must also be possible for the law to change as society develops and changes. The legal system attempts to achieve those two conflicting aims.

Parliament and the law

Laws made by Parliament are supreme over all other law in Britain including law decided by the courts. Acts of Parliament start their life as Bills which are discussed by both the House of Commons and the House of Lords. Bills are usually amended by the two Houses and then become binding at a date decided by Parliament. The law making process does not stop there. Most Acts contain provisions for making Regulations which deal with matters that need to be laid down with greater precision and detail than is needed in the Act itself. Government Ministers promote this type of delegated legislation which will itself have to be approved by Parliament. And in some types of legislation Ministers or others are given power to give directions which are themselves legally binding. We have no written constitution so Parliament can always change or repeal laws it has itself made.

The courts and the law

Courts were for centuries the main law makers. A system of law was developed from individual cases both in criminal and non-criminal matters. Decisions by judges established precedents which provided principles on which later cases were decided. Only over the last hundred years has the body of law changed significantly because of Parliament's activity. The *precedent system* still dominates in the courts. The higher the court the more important its decisions. So cases decided by the House of Lords bind all other courts. Those decided by the Court of Appeal bind, usually, that court itself and always inferior courts. Cases decided by the High Court will bind County Courts but not other High Court cases. Decisions of magistrates courts, County Courts and Crown Courts will not create law.

How the law is used

All legal problems will contain questions of fact as well as law. You will need to establish the facts of the case first and then decide *how* in the legal system those facts should be treated.

Non-criminal. In fact only a minority of non-criminal legal problems ever reach a court. It is usually possible for the two sides to come to some agreement about facts and how the law should be applied to those facts and then they reach a settlement.

Criminal. You can only be convicted of a crime in a Criminal Court. But you are unlikely to be prosecuted unless the police feel that there is at least some chance of convicting you so they too try to establish the facts of the case before starting proceedings.

When the courts are used most time is spent on each side putting forward its view about the facts of the case. Not much time will be given up to legal arguments. When legal arguments do take place each side will put forward an interpretation of cases which have set precedents or of a particular section of an Act of Parliament. The judge will have to decide which interpretation is right.

The Burden of Proof in court cases

Our legal system does not insist on establishing absolute truth in every case. We have an adversary system where each side puts its view to the court, and tries to shake the other side's evidence by challenging questioning in the hope of being able to present the most powerful case. The court must base its decision on whether or not the burden of proof has been satisfied. In non-criminal cases for one side to win it must satisfy the court that on the balance of probability its case is right. The burden of proof is higher in criminal cases. For a defendant to be convicted the court has to be sure that he or she committed the crime so the prosecution must prove its case beyond reasonable doubt.

Identifying a legal problem

There is no clear way of identifying legal problems. Everybody knows that the only way of solving some difficulties, like a wish to be divorced, is to use the law. But many people fail to get advice or help with some problems where the law can help. If you are physically hurt in some way you may have a right to sue somebody. If you buy faulty goods you may have a claim against the seller. If you rent a home which is in a bad state you may be able to force the landlord to carry out repairs. Only you can assert your rights but most of us need help and advice to do this.

2 Where to go for Help and Advice

It is not usually easy to get immediate expert advice. Most advisers, and that includes solicitors, do not specialize. They rely on having a general grasp of the subjects about which they are regularly consulted. They look up things they do not know or take advice themselves from an expert. But it is most important to find advisers whom you can trust, who are sympathetic, and who are willing to take some time with your problem. So it is always sensible before seeking advice to ask around your friends to find out where help is available, and something, if possible, about the reputation the adviser has. There are also various obvious places where you can go for legal advice without going straight to a solicitor.

Who provides help and advice

Citizens Advice Bureaux

There are over five hundred Citizens Advice Bureaux (CABs) in the country and you can find your nearest one from the local town hall. The Bureaux keep their knowledge and information up to date through an efficient reference service supplied by their headquarters in London. Some staff are full time and some are voluntary. The voluntary advisers do have to receive some training before they are allowed to give advice so they have some knowledge of all the common problems people have and will give advice, write letters and make phone calls for you.

The better CABs are now taking a more active role – they will act on your behalf as well as tell you what your rights are. Some staff will now represent you in tribunals. If they are unwilling to do this for you, then ask them why. You should

try and persuade them at least to go to the tribunal with you
or ask them if they know anyone in the area who will represent you.

- Some bureaux also have solicitors who come in and help.
These operate a rota system and you will probably need to
make an appointment to see the solicitor who attends at set
times each week. If the staff cannot help you they will usually
refer you to someone who can.

If you are referred somewhere else, make sure you report
back to the CAB on the help you get. If it is not up to scratch
they will want to know.

Town Hall employees

Many local councils have people to give advice on particular
problems such as housing and some now have housing-aid
centres. The majority employ harassment officers whose job
is to deal with illegal or threatened illegal evictions and
harassment. Equally, council employees, such as social
workers, can be very helpful though they are not usually
knowledgeable about the law. At least you can ask them to
put you in touch with someone who can help.

Trade unions and politicians

If you are a member of a trade union you should be able to
get legal advice from your head office about any problem
arising from your work. Most unions will assist you with
problems over national insurance or industrial injury benefit.
If you have been denied unemployment benefit for some reason
they will usually be willing to represent you at a tribunal.
And naturally you should contact your shop steward or
district official. Some unions operate a free legal advice
scheme for every type of problem. MPs and local councillors
who often have weekly 'surgeries' will be able to give advice
or take up your problem, particularly if it concerns central or
local government. Contact the Town Hall or the local
political party to find out where they operate from.

Legal advice centres

There are now many part time legal advice centres, staffed voluntarily by lawyers. They do not usually take cases to courts or tribunals for you, but will write letters and make phone calls. There are a few full time law centres which are like neighbourhood-based solicitors' practices. Again contact the town hall to find out if there is an advice or law centre near you.

Solicitors

The legal profession is divided into two branches, solicitors and barristers. Members of the public have to go to a solicitor to get legal services. Barristers can only be called in by the solicitor although of course the client pays the barrister's bill. You can of course approach a solicitor direct rather than use the agencies described. It's best to ring for an appointment rather than just walk into the office. Solicitors should be able to give advice on all legal questions. They will advise you on your rights, or lack of them, carry out negotiations and arrange settlements. If the problem is difficult they may suggest a barrister should be consulted. Solicitors can appear for you as advocates in magistrates and County Courts and before tribunals. Unfortunately at present most solicitors have little experience of social security matters so you would often do better to consult an advice centre first.

Barristers

Barristers specialize in advocacy. Their major job is to argue your case for you before a court or tribunal. But they also tend to specialize in particular areas of law. So for a criminal problem your solicitor would consult a barrister who works mainly on criminal cases. Barristers appear as advocates in magistrates and County Courts, and appear in the Crown Courts and in the High Court. (See Chapter 3.) All their work comes from solicitors who instruct them to appear in court for you or to give you an opinion on some legal point where the solicitor needs advice or wants a second opinion. QCs are senior barristers who can only appear in court with a junior barrister. So using a QC is very expensive.

How to choose a solicitor

Choosing a solicitor is obviously important. If you do not know of a good one then ask around. Advice centres and CABs should give you a clear guidance on what solicitors to use; do not let them get away with showing you a list and asking you to pick out a name. Insist on a recommendation. A solicitor's name will need to be included in most legal aid forms (see page 31) so it is helpful to have a solicitor's name when filling in the form, particularly in a magistrates court. There is no reason why you should not ring up a solicitor's firm and ask them if they specialize in your particular problem.

Legal fees and costs

You can pay a solicitor privately or use the legal aid scheme if you are eligible (see page 28). The solicitor should be able to give you some idea of what he will charge before starting work for you and it is sensible to ask about this. There are some fixed scale charges, but for most work the solicitor can charge what he wants as long as it is 'reasonable'. You can always challenge a bill and ask the Law Society, the solicitor's trade union, to check it. Write to the Law Society, 122 Chancery Lane, London WC2, as soon as possible, as there are often time limits within which the complaint must be made. If however the bill relates to a court case then you can challenge it in the court.

What are the charges for?

There are nearly always two sorts of charges.

Fees (or disbursements) are money paid for the solicitor's out-of-pocket expenses. They include things like court fees for filing documents, the cost of telephone calls and postage as well as travelling expenses.

Profit costs are the solicitor's charge for the actual work he does and he pays his overheads like salaries and office rent from this as well as making his actual profit out of the work he does. It is impossible here to give any useful guidance as to how much you will have to pay so always remember to ask your solicitor about it.

Costs in court cases

Costs can be very high particularly in court cases. It is usual for the courts to award costs to whichever side wins the case. So if you lose you can find yourself paying both your own legal costs and most of your opponent's as well. However if you have been granted legal aid and lose, the court is less likely to make you pay your opponent's full costs. If that does happen the costs will normally be limited to the amount of contribution you have had to make to the legal aid fund.

Legal aid

The legal aid scheme is designed to provide help in all legal areas for those who cannot afford to pay legal costs. The idea is to make sure that people do not suffer simply because of lack of means. The state contributes to the cost of the legal aid scheme and the rest of the cost is met out of contributions from people who receive help. Much the same principle applies in all the different aspects. You will not get help unless you can satisfy an income and capital test. You may also have to contribute to the solicitor's costs. And sometimes you may be refused help because you are not thought to have a good case.

There are three aspects to the scheme. Legal advice and assistance, civil legal aid and criminal legal aid and these are explained in the following sections.

Legal advice and assistance

What can the solicitor do?

As long as you are financially eligible the solicitor can help you with any legal problem. You do not need to show that it is 'reasonable' you should get advice. So the solicitor can give you verbal advice, write letters for you, negotiate settlements, draft agreements and wills and help you to prepare court or tribunal cases. But he is not normally allowed to appear for you in a court or tribunal. The scheme is known as the 'green form' scheme from the colour of the application form you fill in. Under the scheme the solicitor can do work costing up to £25. If he needs to spend more on your case he has to ask permission from the Law Society. Solicitors do all the necessary administration in their own offices but they can go and give help out of the office so they might visit somebody in prison or go to see a sick person in their home.

Are you financially eligible?

You must satisfy both the following tests:

The capital test. If you have 'disposable capital' of more than £250 you cannot get help. To work out 'disposable capital' take your savings and deduct £125 for a first dependant, £80 for a second and £40 for any other dependants. Houses are assessed as a separate item. If your house is worth less than £6000 after deducting any unpaid part of your mortgage its value is not counted. Nor would your furniture or personal effects be included.

The income test. Anybody who gets supplementary benefit or family income supplement is automatically eligible provided they are under the capital limits. Otherwise you need a disposable income of less than £28·00 a week. To work out your disposable income, take your net weekly earnings after normal deductions then subtract supplementary benefit rates for your dependants. At the moment these are

For a wife . . .	£5·25
Anybody over 18 . . .	£6·70
Children: 16–18 . . .	£5·15
13–15 . . .	£4·35
11–12 . . .	£3·55
5–10 . . .	£2·90
Less than 5 . . .	£2·40

If you live apart from your dependants then you can deduct the amount of maintenance you pay. You cannot deduct rent, rates or hire purchase commitments.

Working out eligibility. The solicitor will do the calculations for you. So if you are in doubt about your eligibility go along and see him and take your last wage slip with you.

The contribution. If you have more than the disposable capital then you cannot get help. If your disposable income is under £28·00 a week then you are eligible but may have to make a contribution on the following scale:

Between £26·01 and £28·00 – £21·00
   £24·01 and £26·00 – £18·00
   £22·01 and £24·00 – £15·00
   £20·01 and £22·00 – £12·00
   £18·01 and £20·00 – £9·00
   £16·01 and £18·00 – £6·50
   £15·01 and £16·00 – £4·00
   £14·01 and £15·00 – £1·50

If you receive supplementary benefit or family income supplement you can get help free, provided you satisfy the capital test.

Paying the contribution. The solicitor will usually ask for the contribution when he first sees you. But he might agree to accept payment by instalments, so ask him. Also you may not have to pay the full contribution if the cost of the advice is less. If it is more, the solicitor gets the rest of his costs from the legal aid fund. Always ask how much the solicitor thinks the work he is going to do will cost.

Winning your case. There is not much for free in the legal aid scheme. So if you win some money or preserve a right to some property the solicitor may have a right to make up his costs out of this. Technically he has what is called a charge on the property recovered or preserved. The charge will not apply to maintenance or benefit payments or to some other things.

Once again ask about the prospects of this charge being imposed.

Civil legal aid for court cases

Some non-criminal cases cannot be settled by simply nego-tiating and writing letters. Court proceedings will often need to be started by you or may have been started against you. It still often happens that the case is settled before it gets into a court. But if your solicitor thinks you need to start a court case or somebody has started one against you, then legal aid can be obtained through the Law Society. The only exception to this is for non-criminal cases (such as matrimonial disputes and problems concerning children) which are fought out in magistrates courts. Here legal aid is obtained through the court.

Applying for civil legal aid

You need to fill in a fairly long and complicated form and it is best to ask the solicitor to do this. You or the solicitor give details of the case you want to start, or have to defend. You also give brief details of your income. The form is sent to the Law Society who send off the income details to the Depart-ment of Health and Social Security (DHSS). They normally call you for an interview unless you are on social security and find out about your income (see below for financial eligibility). When the DHSS have assessed your income and decided you are financially eligible they inform the Law Society.

The reasonableness test. If you are financially eligible a com-mittee of solicitors and barristers then considers whether it is 'reasonable' to give you legal aid. If they decide it is, you are sent a form to sign and any contribution you make is usually payable monthly. Once you have legal aid the solicitor cannot charge you any more money. He claims his costs and the costs of a barrister if one is used from the Law Society. But you have to pay your contributions. This whole process can take anything from two to four months, though emergency cases can be dealt with quite quickly.

Are you financially eligible?

You must satisfy both the capital and the income tests otherwise you will not get legal aid. If you do satisfy the tests then you may or may not have to make a contribution to your solicitor's costs.

Husband, wife and children. Normally the income and capital of a husband and wife living together are combined when working out eligibility. This does not apply if the case is a dispute between husband and wife. If a child is a party to the case then the assessment will be made on his or her parents' income.

The capital test. If you have more than £1200 'disposable capital' you will not normally get legal aid. To work this out take your savings and deduct £125 for your first dependant, £80 for the next and £40 for every other dependant. If your home is worth less than £6000 after paying the mortgage then its value is not counted nor is your furniture or personal effects. If your disposable capital is less than £250 you do not have to make any contribution. If it is more, then generally you have to contribute up to the likely maximum cost of your case.

The income test. The table below shows how to work out your disposable income:

ADD the following

£. p

Husband and wife's earnings after tax
   and insurance
Family allowance
Family income supplement
Any other income

TOTAL A ...

ADD the following

£.　p

Supplementary scale rates for dependants
(as on page 30)

Rent and rates
Mortgage repayments
Employment expenses
£2 general expenses

TOTAL B . . .

Deduct total B from total A and multiply by 52. This gives your disposable income. If it is over £1380 you will not be eligible; if it is below that then deduct £440 and divide the result by three to find your maximum contribution.

Example: If your 'disposable capital' works out at £270 you will be asked to contribute £20. If your disposable income is £554 the contribution may be £38, i.e. £554 − £440 = £114 divided by 3 = £38.

The contribution: Remember these calculations give only a rough guide. When in any doubt you should claim. The Law Society do not always automatically charge the maximum contribution in every case. The figure they ask you to pay when they send you the form offering you legal aid may be less than the one you have worked out because they do not think the case will be very expensive.

Winning your case

If you win your case and are awarded costs against the other side, then the whole sum goes to the legal aid fund and the money is used to pay your solicitor. Sometimes the Law Society will take your costs from any money you receive or from property you preserve in the case. This is known as the charge. It will not apply to some things you win like maintenance payments. You can be ordered to pay the other side's costs by the court if you lose, although this is unusual. If this happens it will be in addition to your contribution but will not usually be greater than it.

B

Appeals against a refusal of civil legal aid

If the Law Society decide your income or capital is too high you cannot appeal. But if they seem to have made a mistake about this you should ask your solicitor to have your assessment re-checked by the DHSS. However if the Law Society say it is not reasonable for you to take the case then you can appeal to an 'area committee'. But the appeal must be within 4 days so you must appeal immediately. You, or preferably your solicitor, may go along and argue why you should get legal aid before a committee of solicitors and barristers. A high percentage of these appeals are successful.

Changes in income or capital

If you have been awarded legal aid and your income or capital changes, you must tell the Law Society. They may ask for a reassessment of your contribution. That can obviously either increase or decrease the contribution.

Civil Cases in Magistrates Courts

Applications for legal aid in these cases (usually matrimonial disputes, or affiliation or guardianship cases) are made direct to the magistrates court. Again a form has to be completed but this is handed to the court clerk who, with the magistrates, can grant legal aid. The income test is done by the DHSS but usually after the case has finished.

Criminal Legal Aid

If you are accused of a crime it is often vital to be represented in court, particularly if you wish to plead not guilty. The legal aid scheme for criminal cases is operated by the magistrates and Crown Courts. If you get legal aid it covers representation by a solicitor and sometimes a barrister.

Applying for criminal legal aid

Application is made on a long form. The important question is why do you want legal aid and you should fill that in in some detail. For instance, if it is a serious case which could adversely affect your reputation you should say so. The court then considers whether or not the interests of justice require that you should be given legal aid. The application can be granted by a legal aid clerk – but *he* cannot refuse it. If he is doubtful he must show the application to the magistrate who can grant the application or refuse it. Applications can also be made verbally on any appearance in court, and if granted by the magistrate you will then need to fill in the form.

Financial eligibility. Unlike civil legal aid there is no maximum income or capital limit. But you have to give details of your income and capital and you can be required to make a down payment of usually about £5 or £10. Because it is important to get cases on quickly, the financial contribution, if any, is assessed at the end of the case. You will not have to pay anything if you receive supplementary benefit or if you have a very low income and virtually no savings.

The contribution. A contribution is not always required, although it depends on all the circumstances. Somebody who has been sent to prison is unlikely, for instance, to be able to pay a contribution. The court can decide to ask for a contribution but leave the amount to be assessed by the DHSS in the same way as for civil cases. When the DHSS has done the financial test the court will then make an order for payment, either in a lump sum or by instalments.

Refusal of criminal legal aid. There is no appeal against a refusal to grant legal aid, but you can always apply again. It's best to try to get a solicitor to apply in the court on your behalf. If your case is going to a Crown Court then you can apply to that court if the magistrates have refused to grant you legal aid. In magistrates courts unless the case is particularly serious, the legal aid will only cover a solicitor's costs, and not those of a barrister. In the Crown Court the legal aid covers a solicitor's and barrister's costs as well as advice about an appeal if you are convicted.

Bad advice and what to do

If you think you have been badly advised by a lawyer you can complain to the Law Society, 122 Chancery Lane, London WC2, for solicitors, or the General Council of the Bar, Temple, London EC4, for barristers. You have to put your complaint in writing and it will have to be a complaint of professional misconduct for anything to be done. Barristers and solicitors can be disciplined for not behaving properly and in extreme cases can be refused permission to practise. Neither happens very often.

The other problem which most often arises is a complaint that your solicitor or barrister has been negligent. You will have to show that they have failed to reach a minimum standard of professional skill and that you suffered loss as a result. It is usually necessary to use another solicitor to sue or negotiate for you and they are often reluctant to take such cases on. You cannot normally sue for negligence which takes place during the handling of court cases nor is wrong advice necessarily negligent. All solicitors are insured against negligence claims and when you have a good case it will normally be settled before coming to court.

3 Civil and Criminal Courts

Courts are essential for providing a relatively impartial system of settling disputes. Court cases can be disputes about facts or about the law or about both. Most courts have to decide what the facts are after hearing evidence. They then apply the law to those facts and reach a decision. The vast majority of disputes, particularly in civil cases, never come anywhere near a court but they are settled between the two sides on legal principles which the courts have helped to establish. Civil cases are those where there is no accusation of crime. Criminal courts deal with people accused of breaking the criminal law.

What do Civil Courts deal with?

These courts deal with disputes involving individuals, companies and government offices. There are three main types of courts where civil cases can be started.

County Courts

What cases do County Courts deal with?

The country is divided into County Court districts and, broadly, each County Court deals with disputes which arise in its particular district. They have power to deal with cases which involve no more than £1000 unless both sides agree that the limit can be ignored. Most cases in the County Courts concern debts owed by people to such organizations as hire purchase companies. In addition they can try landlord and tenant cases, undefended divorce cases, and various other types of actions, whatever the amount of money involved.

Judges and staff of the County Court

These courts have full time judges who are highly qualified lawyers. They wear wigs and robes when hearing cases. In addition all County Courts have a registrar who is also a qualified lawyer. He acts as an assistant judge in cases which involve less than £75 and often in landlord and tenant disputes whatever the sum involved. One of his most important jobs is to settle preliminary aspects of cases before they go to the judge. The chief clerk of the court and his staff administer the court offices, deal with questions and enquiries from people, and ensure that all the necessary forms and papers are properly completed by litigants.

Is your case a 'Small Claims' case?

It can be both expensive and time consuming to sue in the County Court. But it is cheaper and relatively quick if your claim is for less than £75. These are known as 'small claims'. It's sensible to take legal advice before starting an action like this yourself, but it is cheaper to carry out the case without a solicitor. The procedure for small claims has recently been much improved. You can now get a useful booklet from the court showing you how to proceed as well as standard forms from the court which are easy to complete when you start your case. You have to put in the names of both sides, what the claim is for, and how much money is involved. The registrar hears small claims cases in an informal manner. He can also be asked to act as an arbitrator rather than as a judge so the issues can be settled speedily. If the small claims procedure does not apply in your case then you may need the help of a solicitor.

How County Court cases are started

Cases are started by one party known as the plaintiff asking at the court to issue a summons against the defendant. The plaintiff has to complete an application form, called a *praecipe*, which sets out details of the defendant and a short statement of the claim. In addition the plaintiff has to provide two

copies of a detailed 'particulars of claim', which ought to be
written out before going to issue the summons. He pays a court
fee for the issue of the summons and an extra fee if he wants
the court bailiff to serve it. It is best to get the bailiff to serve the
summons as otherwise you have to swear an 'affidavit of service'
if you serve it yourself. If you do this take advice from a clerk at
the court. A 'particulars of claim' will look something like this:

In the Yorkshire County Court　　　　　Plaint No. . . . .

Between
　　　　Samuel Egar　　　　Plaintiff
　　　　　　and
　　　　Harriet Griffin　　　　Defendant

Particulars of claim
1) I am the owner of Flat 1, 10, Hunt Road, Eye, Yorks, which is let
   furnished to Miss Griffin on a weekly tenancy for £5 a week.
2) By notice to quit dated 4th January 1974 expiring on the 1st
   February gave notice to Miss Griffin.
3) By a decision of the Eye Rent Tribunal dated 21st February 1974
   Miss Griffin's security of tenure was extended to the 21st June
   1974. No further application for extension has been made by her.
4) The rateable value of the property is under £400.
5) The rent has not been paid since the 26th April 1974
   And I now claim
   1. Possession of Flat 1, 10, Hunt Road, Eye, Yorks.
   2. Unpaid rent £40.
   3. Mesne profits at £5 a week since 24th June 1974.
   4. Costs.

Dated 17th July 1974

To the Registrar and to the　　　　Signed S. Egar,
　　　Defendant.　　　　　　　　Flat 2, 10, Hunt Road,
　　　　　　　　　　　　　　　Eye, Yorks, where service of
　　　　　　　　　　　　　　　all proceedings will be
　　　　　　　　　　　　　　　accepted by the plaintiff.

Defending a claim in the County Court

If you are the defendant once you are served with a summons
you must respond to it within the time limit given on it,
usually 14 days. You have various alternatives.

1. You can admit the claim for whatever it may be. That will mean you have to pay over any money claimed or, in the case given above, accept that the plaintiff has a right to evict you. It will also limit the costs which are usually awarded to the winning side.

2. You can deny the claim and say you wish to defend it.

3. You can put in a counterclaim for something from the plaintiff.

It is very important to get legal advice before doing any of these things but do it well within the time limit or you might find the plaintiff has entered judgement against you because of your failure to respond. A defence to the case given above might look something like this:

In the Yorkshire County Court   Plaint No............

Between

       Samuel Egar   Plaintiff
           and
       Harriet Griffin   Defendant

Defence:

1. The only furniture provided by Mr Egar is a bed, a table and five chairs. Therefore the amount of rent which can fairly be attributed to the use of the furniture is not substantial in relation to the whole rent, even taking into account the value of the use of the furniture to me.

2. The rent is unpaid because Mr Egar refuses to accept it.

     Counterclaim:

I claim damages limited to £200 against Mr Egar because he has failed to repair the roof of the house and consequently in heavy rain it leaks into my bedroom causing me inconvenience and damaging my clothes.

To the Registrar   Dated: 25 July 1974
and to the Plaintiff.   Signed H. Griffin
                             Flat 1, 10, Hunt Road

You would have to send two copies to the court and keep one for yourself. Or you can use the form sent out by the court in which case make sure you keep a copy of what you write.

The usual steps in a County Court case

If the case is to be fought, you or your lawyer will be given a hearing date by the Registrar. There may be a pre-trial review at the County Court when the issues are clarified by the registrar before the case goes to the judge. He will also make orders giving time limits in which defences and other documents have to be served. It is common in County Court cases for each side to inspect the other's documents so a set of documents can be agreed for use at the trial. You will always need to consider whether to try to arrange a settlement to avoid too many costs and in addition what witnesses might be needed to help your side.

What happens at the hearing

Once the case finally comes to court for hearing the procedure is quite standard. The judge presides in his wig and gown and has a clerk sitting in front of him. The plaintiff or his lawyer starts off by outlining the facts and the law as he sees them. The plaintiff will usually then give evidence on oath by answering questions from his own lawyer. The defendant or his lawyer then cross-examines. After he has finished, the plaintiff or the plaintiff's lawyer can re-question on anything which has come up in the cross-examination. The same procedure is followed for any other witnesses the plaintiff has. The judge himself will often ask questions of the witnesses.

When all the witnesses have given evidence the defence starts. Their case is either outlined in the same way, or the defendant and his witnesses immediately give evidence on oath, are cross-examined by the plaintiff's side and re-examined, if necessary. If the defence gives evidence first the

lawyer will usually make a speech at the end of the evidence.
The plaintiff's side has the opportunity to reply to the defence
evidence. The judge then summarizes the case and decides for
one of the two sides. He should also be asked by the winning
side to make an order for costs in their favour. A judgement
is drawn up by the court and a copy is sent later to both
sides.

Appeals

The side which has lost may have a right of appeal. Appeals
are of course costly and if you lose you may well have to
pay the other side's costs as well as your own. You should
take legal advice before appealing.

Appeals from the registrar. You can appeal from a judgement
of the registrar to the County Court judge who considers the
grounds of appeal and the evidence, given this time on sworn
statements rather than in person. The appeal has to be lodged
at the court within 14 days of the judgement being made. He
can overrule the registrar, confirm his decision, vary it or
order a re-hearing.

Appeals from the judge. If the judge has given a decision you
are dissatisfied with then any appeal is heard by the Court of
Appeal sitting at the High Court in the Strand in London.
Appeals can be based on the judge misinterpreting the law
and in rare cases on the ground that he came to a wrong
decision on the facts. The appeal has to be lodged within six
weeks.

How long do County Court cases take?

The simplest cases take no more than two or three weeks
from the time the proceedings are issued to the judgement.
Complicated cases can take months before the final hearing.
The following check list shows the main stages and gives a
general idea of the time each step has to take:

1. Issue of ordinary summons by plaintiff:

Registrar will fix a hearing date or a date for pre-trial review within 3 to 6 weeks.

2. Issue of a default summons.

Judgement can be obtained by the plaintiff within 14 days of service of the summons on the defendant unless a defence is put in.

3. Defence:

This will usually have to be put in to the court within 14 days of the service of the summons.

4. Request for further and better particulars.

The defendant can ask the plaintiff for more detailed information about the points made by him in his summons. You must usually reply within 7 days.

5. Preparation of lists of documents and inspection of them.

It is normal to exchange lists of documents within 7 days of the defence being filed. Each side then looks at the other's documents within 7 days of the exchange.

6. Trial:

The registrar will fix a date either when the summons is issued or at the pre-trial review. It is usually at least 6 weeks away.

7. Judgement.

This is sent within a few days of the court's decision.

What happens after judgement is given?

Unless the case is settled to both sides' satisfaction there will always be a loser in a court case. If you have to pay money then get the judge to allow you to do this by instalments. If you fail to pay, the plaintiff can take further proceedings. The two most common are described below but in addition you can be made bankrupt or have your bank account seized.

Enforcing a judgement

Execution. The plaintiff has to request the court to enforce a judgement. He obtains a warrant from the court and the court bailiff, armed with the warrant, can enter the debtor's home and seize his furniture and other effects. Unless the debtor actually pays the money owed and the court fees the bailiff can sell the goods he has taken at auction. Things that do not belong to you, such as goods being bought on hire purchase, cannot be seized.

Attachment of earnings. This is becoming a very common method of getting a judgement debt paid. The plaintiff applies to the court for an attachment of earnings summons. Within 14 days of being served with the summons the debtor has to give details of his income. The court can also demand details from the debtor's employer. A private hearing then takes place before the registrar. He decides how much the debtor needs to meet his weekly commitments and how much he can afford to pay each week to reduce the debt. The employer is then ordered to deduct that money weekly from the debtor's wages and he sends it to the court.

Court costs

If you find you have to pay the other side's costs, or if you are on legal aid, the costs will be 'taxed' by the court. That means the solicitor draws up his bill and has it vetted by the registrar and the other side if they want to be involved. This process can take a considerable time.

Magistrates courts

A description of how these courts are organized appears in the criminal courts section as their main work is in the criminal law. But magistrates also hear licensing cases (such as applications for pub licences) and deal with family matters. They then sit as either Licensing Justices or as a domestic bench and no criminal cases appear in their lists. The way the domestic bench works is described in the section on breakdown of marriage (see page 59). But in addition, magistrates courts can make guardianship orders if they think necessary.

That could happen if both parents were dead or the court decided that a parent was unfit to have charge of a child.

The High Court

The High Court is divided into three divisions. The *Queen's Bench Division* handles contracts, personal injury and damages cases. The *Family Division* deals with divorces, adoptions and other matrimonial cases. The *Chancery Division* hears cases of wills, trusts, company matters and tax.

Broadly, High Court cases involve disputes which cannot be heard in the County Court because of the money limits, or cases which the plaintiff considers merit the increased costs of using the High Court system. The various Divisions also hear appeals from magistrates courts and tribunals. High Court judges travel around the country and hear claims for damages, defended divorces and large money claims but much High Court work is done in London.

The preliminary and trial procedure is much the same as in the County Court but it isreally essential to be represented by lawyers in actions in any of the Divisions. Appeals from High Court judges go to the Court of Appeal in London and it is possible to appeal from that court to the House of Lords.

Criminal Courts

These courts deal with people who are charged with breaking the criminal law. The two main types are the magistrates court and the Crown Court. All criminal cases start at a local level in either a magistrates or a juvenile court. The case may finally be dealt with at a Crown Court or after appeal in the High Court, Court of Appeal or House of Lords.

Magistrates and juvenile courts dealing with crimes

The whole country is divided into magistrates courts districts; people charged with offences appear before the magistrates or the juvenile court for the area where the offence took place. Magistrates are either unpaid lay people who are usually of some standing locally or in large cities there are some full time legally qualified magistrates called stipendiaries. There are normally three magistrates on the bench, although stipendiaries sit on their own. A clerk sits below the magistrates. He is legally qualified and advises the bench on the law although he should give them no advice on what evidence to believe. The court staff deal with administration. There are police officers attached to all magistrates courts and they are present at most hearings.

What type of cases are dealt with by magistrates?

Magistrates do not deal with every case. If the case is too serious to be tried by them, they can commit the accused person for trial to the Crown Court (see page 47). The accused person can in some cases elect to be tried by the Crown Court. Magistrates can send a person they find guilty for sentence to that court.

How do you come before a magistrates court?

People come before the court in two ways. They can be summonsed in writing by the court after they have heard brief details of the offence from the prosecution, usually the police. Or they can be arrested, charged and brought before the court the next day. If you are charged with an offence or summonsed then you should consult a solicitor unless you consider the case really trivial. Conviction of a criminal offence can adversely affect you all your life, as well as resulting in a punishment which could include prison. A solicitor can tell you whether you have been properly charged; he will know if any technical defences are open to you and will be able to prepare your case so as to present it in its best light. Legal aid may be available to pay for this (see page 34).

Deciding whether to plead guilty or not guilty

It may be a difficult decision as to whether you should plead guilty or not as even if you are innocent you may have difficulties in persuading the court that you are. But once you have decided to plead not guilty then your case needs careful preparation. You may need an adjournment to enable you to do this and you should apply for that as well as asking for bail and legal aid (see pages 34 and 113). Witnesses should be approached, and if they are not willing to come, but you need them as witnesses, then a witness summons should be obtained from the court.

Committal for trial to a Crown Court

You may in some cases decide to be tried by judge and jury at the Crown Court or the case may go there automatically or on request by the prosecution. If the case is to go higher, the magistrates have to be satisfied that there is a case to answer. They decide this by the prosecution outlining its case either orally or in writing. But if you can decide on whether to go before a jury you should take advice. You may have a better chance of persuading a jury you are innocent than of persuading the magistrates.

Trial procedure in the magistrates court

If you are tried by the magistrates, the procedure is always the same. You have to appear at a specified time in the morning or afternoon and your case will be listed on the court notice boards. When the court starts to hear your case you will be called and the charge is read out to you. You will be asked to plead guilty or not guilty. Should you plead guilty the prosecution then summarizes the facts of the case and tells the court of any previous convictions. You can call character witnesses and make a speech in mitigation in the hope of persuading the magistrates to be lenient. They will pass sentence or send you to a higher court for sentence if they think the case is serious.

If you plead not guilty then the prosecution outlines the facts of the case and calls witnesses who give evidence on oath. The witnesses give evidence in reply to questions from the prosecution lawyer. You, or your lawyer, can cross-examine them and should challenge any part of their story you disagree with. The prosecution can re-examine on any matters which come out in cross-examination. When the prosecution evidence is finished the defence has two choices. You can make a submission of 'no case to answer'. This means the defence attempts to persuade the court that there is not sufficient evidence for you to need to make any answer to the charge. If you do not make this submission, or if it fails, you call your witnesses. In most cases, the defendant himself should give evidence first, although there is no obligation to do so. Then *you* can call any other witnesses. The same process of questions by your side, cross-examination and re-examination takes place as for the prosecution case. At the end of your evidence you, or your lawyer, should make a final speech to the bench summing up the evidence and distinguishing any facts which do not help you.

The magistrate's verdict. Once the case is finished the magistrates confer about their decision. If you are found not guilty you are discharged. If they find you guilty then the same procedure follows omitting the summary of facts by the prosecution as happens immediately after a plea of guilty.

After the verdict. Magistrates courts can fine up to £400 or imprison you for up to 6 months on each charge. The maximum in any event is 12 months, regardless of how many charges are tried together. They will also decide if you should pay any of the prosecution costs. Whether you are found guilty or innocent they can order you to contribute to your legal aid costs if you have had legal aid. If you are found n nocent you can apply for costs against the prosecution.

Appeals

You have a right of appeal within 14 days to the Crown Court against either conviction or sentence or both and are entitled to advice about this if you have had legal aid. If you dispute the decision on a point of law you can get the magistrates to state a case to the Divisional Court of the Queen's Bench Division. Take advice before asking them to do that.

Crown Courts

What cases do Crown Courts deal with?

Any criminal case not tried in a magistrates court is heard in a Crown Court before a judge and jury. These courts are usually in large cities but they are held elsewhere as needed. Appeals are heard without a jury. The procedure is the same as in magistrates courts, but it is always advisable to be represented. The court can impose up to the maximum sentence fixed by the law depending on the type of case.

Appeals from Crown Courts

Appeals can be against the conviction or the sentence or both and they go to the Court of Appeal Criminal Division. You can get advice automatically if you are on legal aid. But your appeal is treated as an application for leave to appeal and is usually first considered by a single judge without an oral hearing. If the judge refuses the application you can renew it to two more judges. If they refuse to grant leave to appeal there is no further appeal. Should leave be granted you will normally be given legal aid and your case is argued before the Court of Appeal by a barrister. The only appeal from there is to the House of Lords, if the case concerns a point of law of general public importance and you need permission of the Court of Appeal or the House of Lords to get there. Once all your avenues of appeal are exhausted your only chance of getting the conviction quashed is by the Home Secretary referring the case back to the Court of Appeal or recommending the Queen to grant a pardon. This happens very rarely.

The Rules of Evidence

The rules of evidence apply in all the courts discussed in this chapter. They are designed to make sure that every case is fairly tried and to exclude evidence which cannot be tested in cross-examination. Some of the more important points to remember are set out below:

The rule against leading questions. When you or your lawyer are questioning witnesses for your own side you cannot ask 'leading questions'. This means that you must not give the answer you expect to your question in the question itself. So if you expect a witness to say he was in James Street at 11.00 a.m. on 22 July you would have to ask 'Where were you at 11.00 a.m. on 22 July?' 'Were you in James Street at 11.00 a.m. on 22 July?' would be a leading question. You can however ask leading questions when cross-examining witnesses from the other side.

The rule against hearsay evidence. Basically this means that you are not generally allowed to say things you have heard at second-hand. So if you try to say that Mr Gunn told you that Mrs Kendall had told him she was in James Street at 11.00 a.m. the court will rule out that evidence as being hearsay. Mr Gunn could tell the court about what Mrs Kendall said to him but you cannot. Perhaps the most important exceptions to the rule against hearsay is that confessions are admissible.

The rule against evidence of previous convictions. One important safeguard in criminal cases is that the court must not know if an accused person has a previous criminal record. It would probably prejudice them if they did. The one exception to this rule is if the accused person, or his lawyer, claims that he has a good character and relies on that to help his case. If he does that and in fact has criminal convictions then the prosecution can tell the court about them.

4 Tribunals

Not all disputes are settled in courts. Anybody who disagrees with a decision of the relevant official in supplementary benefit, national insurance, industrial injury or rating cases has a right to appeal to an independent tribunal. Similarly if you think you are paying too high a rent to your landlord you can have your rent settled by a tribunal. If you are a furnished tenant then you may be able to have your security of tenure extended by a rent tribunal. And anybody who thinks they have been unfairly sacked or refused redundancy pay can refer the case to an industrial tribunal. Most tribunals either deal with disputes between individuals and government departments, or between private citizens or companies.

Starting an appeal. All appeals to tribunals need to be in writing and it is sensible to take advice from a solicitor or advice centre before starting. When putting in an appeal in cases concerning state benefits, it is very helpful to set out your grounds in full. You need only say 'I wish to appeal' if you want to, but if you say why, then at least your side of the case is set out for the tribunal to consider when they read the case papers before the hearing. In other types of tribunals where you are against another person or a company, you start the case by completing a standard form obtainable from the particular tribunal. You should find the address from your CAB or the phone book. Unless the form asks you to set out the grounds for the appeal, there is no need to do so.

Once the appeal has been lodged the clerk of the tribunal will set a date for the hearing.

Preparation of your case. You need to know precisely what decision you want the tribunal to make. To win the case, you should firstly be able to summarize the history of your benefit claim or of your relationship with the other side. Secondly, you want, if possible, evidence of witnesses to support your case. Thirdly, you need to relate the facts and the evidence to the law if there are legal issues involved. So if you are appearing on your own it is best to make clear notes of what you want and what evidence you propose to produce. In cases where a government department is involved as the opposition, you will be sent a set of papers prior to the hearing. These will contain the decision appealed against, your appeal statement and a summary of the facts and some observations on why the decision has been reached by the official involved. Your final preparation can be done in the light of those papers. In other types of tribunal all you will get will be a copy of your appeal and the forms completed by your opponent. It is less easy to know what case the other side will put up from these papers.

If you intend to call witnesses or have them send written evidence, you must arrange that. The tribunals have no power to force witnesses to attend. It is always worth asking for an adjournment of the hearing if you are not ready to put your case on the day. Write to the Clerk of the Tribunal, or telephone him. If necessary you can ask for the adjournment at the hearing itself.

Procedure at the hearing. Tribunals are more informal than ordinary courts. The chairman should explain how the tribunal works before the hearing starts but all of them follow a similar pattern. Normally the appellant starts by giving his case. You should summarize very briefly what decision you want, outline the history of the case, give your evidence and get your witnesses to speak, and finish by summarizing what decision you want once again. The other side then gives its case in the same sort of way. The members of the tribunal ask questions whenever they want, but try not to let that divert you from the argument you are putting. Similarly the other side will ask questions of you or your witnesses after each of you have had your say. If they interrupt, suggest to the tribunal that they should ask their question when you have finished. You have a chance to ask the other side and their witnesses any questions after they have given their view of the case. At the end you ought to summarize your case again and try to distinguish or criticize any points the other side has brought up which you feel damage your case.

The decision and appeals from it. Some tribunals give their decision to you immediately after the hearing, others send it by post. You should always consider or take advice on whether to appeal. Some tribunals are not obliged to give reasons for their decision unless you ask them to. So check with the clerk about this and then ask for a reasoned decision if you need to as it helps when deciding whether to appeal further. You must remember there is a time limit on appealing in all cases and though this limit can sometimes be extended if you show 'good cause' you cannot rely on that.

Costs and expenses of appealing. It does not cost anything to appeal to any of the tribunals mentioned later. On the other hand if you win you do not get the costs of loss of earnings and suchlike from the other side. In welfare benefits tribunals you will normally get your fares for attending and sometimes loss of earnings.

Representation at tribunals. You are entitled to be represented in nearly all tribunals by anybody you want, including a lawyer. Trade union officials, in particular, and social workers can be very helpful in national insurance and supplementary benefit cases. You can of course take a friend. The legal aid scheme does not allow solicitors to represent you at the hearing but they can give you preliminary advice on how to prepare the case under the scheme. The tribunal ought to help you put your case, but whether you are represented or not, good preparation is the most important thing you can do.

Some important tribunals

Supplementary Benefit Appeal Tribunals

Anybody who is dissatisfied with a decision about their supplementary benefit can appeal within 21 days to the tribunal. Write to your local DHSS office. The tribunal has three independent members, including a chairman, and a clerk. It holds hearings in private and is quite informal. There is no right of appeal, but in some cases the decision can be challenged in the High Court. You need legal advice about that. These tribunals also hear Family Income Supplement appeals. (For further details see *Supplementary Benefit Rights* by Ruth Lister.)

National Insurance Local Tribunals

If you disagree with a decision by an insurance officer over your right to any of the national insurance benefits, including some industrial injury cases, you can appeal in writing within 21 days to the tribunal. Write to your local DHSS office. There are three members, a lawyer chairman, a person who works as an employer and a working people's representative. The hearings are in public though nobody is usually there and the proceedings are informal. You have a right of appeal within 3 months of the decision to the National Insurance Commissioners. Appeal in writing to your local DHSS office.

Medical Boards and Medical Appeal Tribunals

They decide 'disablement questions' by determining what loss of ability to enjoy a normal life you may have suffered as a result of an industrial injury. Cases are usually referred to the Board by an insurance officer but you can ask to have your case assessed if you wish. The Medical Board is usually two doctors who medically examine you and then decide on your 'loss of faculty' by setting a percentage figure on it. The Medical Appeal Tribunal, two doctors and a lawyer chairman, hears appeals from the Board and operates quite formally. You can appeal against their decision within three months to the National Insurance Commissioners if you can show that a question of law is involved.

National Insurance Commissioners

The Commissioners are very experienced lawyers who act as the top appeal tribunal in the national insurance system. So they hear appeals, among many other things, about unemployment and sickness benefit, attendance allowance and industrial injury benefits. They settle difficult questions of fact and law and it helps to be represented by a trade union or lawyer when appearing before them.

Valuation Courts

These tribunals hear appeals, technically called proposals, about rating assessments set by the Inland Revenue Valuation Officer on your home or on offices and industrial premises. There are three people on the tribunal who sit in public and hear your case. You can appeal against their decision within 28 days to the Lands Tribunal. You make a proposal about lowering your rates to the local valuation officer.

Rent Tribunals

They settle reasonable rents of furnished homes, if your landlord lives on the premises. Either the landlord or tenant can apply by completing a form and sending it to your local rent tribunal. The tribunals can also give tenants up to 6 months' security of tenure. The tribunal has a lawyer chairman and two other members, one of whom is usually a surveyor or valuer. They sit in public.

Rent Officers and Rent Assessment Committees

They settle fair rents for unfurnished tenants of private or housing association landlords after application by either landlord or tenant. The rent officer holds consultations after the application is made and sets the rent. The Committee consists of a lawyer chairman and often two valuers as the other members. They hear appeals from rent officers. They sit in public and the proceedings are quite formal. Apply in writing to the local rent officer to fix your rent.

Industrial Tribunals

These tribunals decide cases of unfair dismissal, redundancy and questions on contracts of employment. They are chaired by a lawyer and have representatives from a panel of employers and working people. They operate quite formally, taking evidence on oath. Besides the clerk, a conciliation officer from the Department of Employment is usually present to give the Department's view of the case. Applications need to be in within 6 months of your dismissal whether for redundancy or otherwise. There is an appeal on a question of law to a higher court. Appeal in writing to the Industrial Tribunal, whose address can be obtained from the Department of Employment.

Part Two

Some Common Legal Problems

5 Family Problems

Breakdown of Marriage

Choosing a remedy

When your marriage breaks down you can always come to an informal agreement with your partner on the terms on which you will separate. But informal agreements are difficult to enforce so, if you want to avoid the courts for the moment, you should get a solicitor to draw up a separation deed. The only problem in that, for the future anyway, is that a deed may stop you from claiming your partner has deserted you. Other alternatives are to go to the magistrates court for a separation order or start divorce proceedings, if that is possible. If you have committed adultery the magistrates court cannot normally grant you any order but the divorce court can.

An order from the magistrates does not put an end to your marriage, but it does provide a cheap, quick and private way of getting maintenance, or the custody of your children. It can make a divorce cheaper, since the magistrates will deal with some of the matters which a divorce court considers. It can also be useful for a wife who wants a local council to transfer to her a council house tenancy. If you are technically able to get a divorce, and do not need a court order to get maintenance, it is probably better to take divorce proceedings straight away. A solicitor will advise you on the best way to proceed. Whatever method you choose, judges, magistrates and solicitors are under a duty to consider the possibilities of reconciliation. So you are certain to be asked about this.

What to do in an emergency

If your spouse is assaulting you or pestering you so unbearably that you must get it stopped at once the best way is to start divorce proceedings. As soon as you start you can apply to the court for an order stopping your spouse from molesting you. If this order is given and broken your spouse may be ordered out of the home or even be sent to prison. Magistrates courts are rather slow for emergency actions.

Grounds for getting a magistrates court order

For a wife to get a separation order (technically a non-cohabitation order) it is necessary to show that the husband has committed a matrimonial offence which he cannot justify because of his wife's conduct. The main grounds are:

Desertion. The deserter must intend to bring married life to an end and cause you to separate into two separate households, although not necessarily under separate roofs. For instance it is possible for a husband and wife to remain in the same house but not to share rooms, meals, household duties or finances. If the deserted party is the one who has actually left the home then he or she will have to show that they left because of the other person's conduct. If you have parted by mutual consent or if your conduct forced your spouse to leave then the court will refuse to find desertion. Genuine offers to return which are refused can also end any case for desertion.

Cruelty. You will have to show persistent cruelty by your spouse to get a separation order on this ground. You will need to show some serious conduct which has caused or is likely to cause injury or danger of injury to your health or to the health of a child of the family. Mental cruelty without actual acts of violence can be enough to prove your case. Try to get a letter from your doctor showing injury to your health.

Adultery. It is often not possible to get clear evidence of adultery. However magistrates courts will accept that it has happened if you can produce evidence that your spouse has had inclination and opportunity to commit adultery. So if a man has been out regularly with another woman and spent evenings at her home the court may accept that adultery has taken place.

Neglect to maintain. To get a separation order on this ground a wife will have to show that her husband has deliberately failed to provide reasonable maintenance for her and the children. Husbands have a duty to maintain their wife and children but the magistrates decide what is reasonable maintenance in each particular case.

Other grounds. Regular drunkenness, drug addiction, sexual assaults on a child of the family or having sex while you know you are suffering from venereal disease can all be reasons for getting a separation order.

How to start proceedings

The complaint usually has to be made within six months of the action against which you are complaining. You can go alone or with a solicitor if you are employing one, and make a formal complaint to a magistrate who will then usually issue a summons. The police should be asked to serve it on the other party. The court usually fixes a hearing, which is always in private, within a reasonably short period. You have to prove the offence complained of and there are various defences that can be used. The other party, the defendant, can say you condoned the offence by forgiveness and by living together again. Or the defendant can say you have connived at or ignored the offence. Or the defendant might say your conduct was so bad that you forced him or her to act as in fact happened or that you have yourself committed adultery. These are technical defences and you will need legal help to deal with them. Once you have proved your case, various orders can be made by the court.

What orders can the magistrates make?

Non-cohabitation order. This puts an end to your duty to live together and the order is most often made in adultery or cruelty cases. It will stop you getting a divorce later on the grounds of desertion but is useful otherwise.

Maintenance for the wife. The court can order payment of weekly maintenance of an unlimited amount. But maintenance payments for a wife are not usually very high. Magistrates courts cannot award wives a lump sum capital payment.

Orders relating to children. The court has an overriding duty to consider the children's welfare and can make orders relating to them whether or not a matrimonial offence is proved. The order will relate to 'children of the family'. That means any child of the couple, adopted children and any children who have been accepted as members of the family by the other side. So where a woman has children from a previous marriage who have been accepted and maintained by her second husband the court could order him to pay maintenance for them as well as for his own children.

Maintenance and custody of children. The court can award an unlimited sum of weekly maintenance for each child of the family. They can also give custody of the children to either party regardless of the fault of either side. The main consideration is always what is best for the child. If magistrates do decide to make a custody order they will usually give the other party reasonable access. You should be sure to ask them to do this. If the magistrates think the circumstances are exceptional they can order a child to be taken into care or to be supervised by the council.

The amount of maintenance. The basic principle is that where the husband is the guilty party the wife and children's maintenance should be set so that their living standards do not suffer more than absolutely necessary. Each side's standard of living may have to go down because there will be two homes. But the wife and children's standard should not be obviously lower nor higher than the husband's. The court will usually take a wife's earnings into account. They will however ignore social security payments. The amounts obviously depend on the husband's earnings but £6 for a wife and £3 for each of the children are fairly normal figures.

Enforcing rights of custody and access

If, say, the husband refused to give custody of the children to his wife or denies her access after being ordered to do so by the court then she will have to complain about this to the magistrates court. The court as well as repeating its order can fine the man or send him to prison. If, on the other hand, rights of access are being abused by a husband, the wife can apply to have his rights of access removed or reduced. Obviously the same rules apply if the wife is in the wrong.

Enforcing rights to maintenance

More often problems arise because no maintenance is paid. It is often impractical to chase a defaulting husband, but there are various possibilities. His wife can take out a summons against him. When the case is heard he will be asked about his means. If the wife has a solicitor he will ask the questions, otherwise it is usual for the clerk of the court to do this. The magistrates can adjourn the case on condition that the husband pays regularly. They can also make an attachment of earnings order. In the last resort he can be sent to prison.

Attachment of earnings orders are most useful against men who have relatively steady jobs with reasonably large firms. Casual workers are inclined to change jobs, and small firms to dismiss men who have this order made against them. The order requires the man's employer to deduct a particular sum over and above a minimum amount for subsistence from the man's wages. This can cause administrative problems in small firms. The employer has to send the money to the court. The minimum amount is known as the protected earnings rate. So when the man's wages are short, he pays less and with good overtime he pays more up to the limit of the order. If the man leaves his job both he and the former employer must tell the court.

Cancelling a magistrates court order

Most magistrates court orders can be cancelled if after the
order you commit adultery or recommence living with your
spouse.

Divorce

Only in a few cases can you start divorce proceedings within
three years of your marriage. You would have to show exceptional hardship or exceptional depravity by the other person
before you got permission. But if you want a divorce within
three years of your marriage then go and see a solicitor who
will give detailed advice about your chances. Once you can,
or do, start divorce proceedings you have to show that the
marriage has irretrievably broken down. The matrimonial
offence no longer exists as it still does in magistrates courts, so
the old idea of the guilty party in divorce proceedings has
gone. In many cases now it is not difficult to show grounds
for divorce and there is rarely argument about the divorce
itself. The most difficult problems arise over maintenance and
children and arrangements about money and there are often
disputes over the children.

The evidence needed to get a divorce

The sole ground for divorce is that the marriage has irretrievably broken down. There are only five ways in which you
can show this.

Adultery. You need to show the other person has committed
adultery and you find it intolerable to live with him or her.
You can prove adultery by confession, or by circumstantial
evidence. That would mean showing that your husband or
wife had both inclination and opportunities to commit
adultery. Some people may need to employ detectives to get
evidence of adultery but you should take legal advice before
doing that. Even if you can prove adultery you still have to
convince the divorce court that you find it intolerable to live

with the other person, though this need not be because of the adultery.

Unreasonable behaviour. This ground replaces the old-fashioned cruelty petition. So violence, neglect and mental cruelty will be good evidence of unreasonable behaviour. You no longer have to show your health has been affected, but it will be strong evidence if you have suffered in this way. It is then necessary to convince the court that you cannot reasonably be expected to live with the other party. So personal factors are vital and these will include your attitude to the other person, your beliefs about why he or she has treated you in the way you complain of and so on.

Desertion. You can show that your marriage has irretrievably broken down if the other party has deserted you for a continuous period of two years before you start the case. The law tries to promote reconciliation so if you have lived together after first separating that will not necessarily put an end to any desertion case. You can live together for one or more periods of up to six months and still prove desertion. But if there have been periods of reconciliation the periods have to be added up so that there has been a full two years of actually living apart before you start the case. So for instance, if you part in January 1973, return together in September 1973, and split up finally in November after two months, you will be able to start divorce proceedings in March 1975. That will be two years and two months since your first separation but you will have had a full two years living apart.

Two year separation. If both parties want a divorce they can show their marriage has irretrievably broken down if they have lived apart for more than two years before starting the case. This is rather like divorce by consent and many divorce cases are now based on this rule.

Five year separation. This ground is in effect divorce without consent. You can get a divorce despite the refusal of the other party to agree, if you have lived apart for five years.

There are special provisions which allow the other party to apply for protection of their financial position.

Arrangements about children and money

If there are no children of the marriage and neither side wants maintenance from the other then divorce is very simple. But in many cases problems will arise about money and who should look after the children. You may not get a divorce finalized until these have been sorted out to the satisfaction of the court.

Providing for children of the marriage

The law is concerned to protect the interests of the children of people who are getting divorced, so when the court makes decisions about custody of the children, access to them and maintenance for them, it is their interests that have first priority not the convenience of the parents. The court will be concerned about children of the family. This means the wife's children by her husband, adopted children and any child who has been treated by both parties as being a member of the family whether or not either side is the child's natural parent. The courts will take into account your children's physical and mental welfare, the conduct of each parent, the children's education, where they are going to live and religious upbringing and then decide on what orders to make about custody and access. If a child is old enough to express a view about who he or she should live with then the court may take that into account.

Usually it is possible to agree about who should look after the children and how often the other person should see them. But if no agreement is reached then there are some general rules. Normally the mother will have the children live with her but a lot depends on who the children have been with and for how long. If the father has had the children for a long time and has a stable home with a housekeeper or if he is soon to be married again then a court might say the children should live with him.

It is very difficult for the father of young children to persuade a court that they should live with him rather than with their mother. It is also unusual for the children to be split up, some living with their father and some with their mother.

Custody and access to children

Technically courts can make orders about custody care and control and access.

A custody order gives parental rights and allows the parent to take decisions about things like education and religious upbringing.

Care and control orders say who the child should live with and will usually give access to the other parent at reasonable times. It is quite common for the parents to have joint custody and for the children to live with one of the parents most of the time.

Disputes can arise after these matters have been settled particularly over access and either parent can go back to the court and complain. In the end disobedience of court orders, contempt of court, can mean being sent to prison.

Maintenance for the children

The husband will normally be required to maintain the children and the amount depends on the needs of the children, previous living standards and the husband's earnings. The parents' responsibility for the breakdown of the marriage is irrelevant. Wealthy people can be made to provide a lump sum settlement.

Orders about maintenance can always be varied if circumstances change. Difficulties arise when a man re-marries and has a second family but in general the courts will insist as far as possible that the interest of the children of the first marriage should not be ignored despite the man's obligations to keep two families. If a wife re-marries her new husband will not be obliged automatically to maintain the children of the previous marriage.

Maintenance normally stops when the child leaves school.

Maintenance orders ought to be registered in magistrates courts which make it easier to collect the money – if the former husband fails to pay, you can get an attachment of earnings order reasonably easily.

Maintenance for the wife

A former wife can get maintenance or a lump sum from her husband. The amount depends on such things as the financial position of each person, their conduct during marriage, how long they were married, and the contributions they each made to the family. A wife will nearly always get maintenance if she has the children of the family to look after but may get none at all if there is no family.

Family property

If you cannot agree on how to divide up family property including any house you own, the court will decide. The judge will look at what contribution has been made by each person, both financially and in other ways – particularly a housewife's contribution to the running of the home. He will try to share out the property fairly but if he cannot do that he will order a sale and a division of the proceeds.

Procedure in divorce cases

You can do all the necessary work yourself but it is better and usually necessary if there are any complications to use a solicitor. Legal aid is of course available to help with the costs (see page 31).

1. The divorce is started by a petition in a special form which is filed in the local Divorce County Court or at the main Divorce Registry, Somerset House, in London. It gives information about the date and place of the marriage, the children's names and their birthdays and the points on which you intend to rely to show your marriage has irretrievably broken down. A separate statement is needed if there are

children of the family, stating what financial and custody arrangements are proposed by you.

2. The petition is then served by the court on the other party. He or she then has to decide whether to oppose the petition and whether to dispute any of the financial or custody arrangements suggested.

3. If you want to defend on any issue, then take legal advice. More often than not a compromise on all relevant points is reached between the parties or their solicitors before the case is heard. At the hearing the petitioner gives evidence on oath and provided the judge is satisfied there are proper grounds he will make a decree nisi. Three months after that, unless there are pressing reasons for hurrying it up, the decree is made absolute. Arrangements about custody of children, maintenance for them and the wife, and the sharing out of family property can if disputed take a long time to settle. The judge may make temporary orders to preserve the position until everything is finally sorted out.

4. If all is agreed before the case, and the judge approves the agreement, he will make the necessary orders when giving the decree nisi. Otherwise all these arrangements will be decided in private hearings before the judge. Once a petition is filed, and as long as agreement is reached between the parties quickly, cases should be heard within about two to four months of getting ready for the trial of the case (depending on how busy the court is).

Problems with Children

Parents have to look after their children. It can be a criminal offence not to do this. They must feed them, clothe them, get them medical help when they are ill and they must not injure them purposely or punish them excessively. But children have no right to enforce parental duties in the courts. Somebody, usually their mother, must do this for them. Problems can arise when there are disputes between parents or neglect by them or the child gets into trouble through his own conduct. There can be difficulties too over schooling, and these are looked at in the following sections:

Disputes between parents

Disputes about how children should be looked after will often arise when the parents themselves have fallen out. The courts may have to deal with it in the long run by granting separation or divorce orders as described in the previous section and by giving custody to one parent who then makes the decisions. The father, as the law stands at present, has the right to decide on religious and educational upbringing unless the mother challenges this and gets an order from the magistrates or the divorce court.

The local authorities role

Local authorities have a duty to ensure that children in need of care and protection are looked after. They also have to try and keep families together; so they should not take children into care when, for instance, the family is homeless. They should be pressed to provide a temporary home. But sometimes children will be taken into care by local authorities either under a voluntary arrangement or compulsorily.

You can ask the council to take over the care of your children if for instance you feel unable to manage because of illness. Go and see the social services department about this. Or the council might decide to take your child into care because they think you are not looking after him or her properly. They have to write to you about this and if you consent they take over your parental rights and duties. If you object then your case has to go to the local magistrates court. If your case gets to court in this way, or if your child is taken to court as being in need of care and control, the court can put your child into the care of the local authority.

You can get your child out of a voluntary care arrangement simply by telling the council you want to do this. But the council could then try and make the care order compulsory. Compulsory orders end usually at 18 or earlier if the council

want to end the arrangement. Children in care will be looked
after in children's homes or by a foster mother.

Children in trouble

Many children run into trouble with the police either because
they are suspected of committing crimes or because they
appear to need care and protection. Children under 10 cannot
be charged with a criminal offence but they can be dealt with
in care proceedings in the same way as outlined above.

The authorities have various choices when dealing with children in trouble.

* They sometimes simply issue a warning about the child's
behaviour, in other words a ticking off.
* Or care proceedings can be taken in the juvenile court if
they decide that the child needs care and protection.
* Or if the matter is considered serious they can prosecute in
the juvenile court. You should get legal help in any court case
and apply for legal aid.

Non-criminal cases in the magistrates courts

If the local council decides your child needs care and protection
whether or not an offence has been committed, they can bring
him or her to the juvenile court. The court has to be satisfied
the child has an unsatisfactory home and, most usually, that
the parents cannot control the child. They can then make a
care order.

It is very important to attend the court and you should apply
for legal aid. The court has a wide choice of orders that it can
make.

The magistrates can bind over the parents to look after the
child. Or they might make a supervision order whereby a
probation officer visits your family and helps the child. Or
your child can eventually be put compulsorily into care. With
the council this is not normally done until a supervision order
has failed.

The court may well make a care order if your child has been

truanting from school or been convicted of criminal offences in the past or even if he or she is involved with 'bad' friends.

Criminal cases involving children

These can be dealt with in the way outlined in the section immediately above, or by criminal prosecution. You should get legal help if your child is to be prosecuted and always go with your child to court, as the magistrates will usually want to talk to you. The offence has to be proved, and then
* the child, or his parents if he is under 14, can be fined or ordered to pay compensation.
* Or the child can be sent to Borstal if he or she is over 15. The magistrates can also make supervision orders or care orders in the same way as when a child is in need of care and protection.

Procedure when children are in trouble with the police

Children can be arrested like anybody else, but should never be questioned except with their parents there or some non-police officer such as a social worker or school teacher who must be of the same sex as the child. They can be questioned at school as long as a teacher is present. Parents may have to insist on these rights. A child must also get bail unless a police inspector decides otherwise. Children under 15 who are not granted bail will be detained in community homes run by the council. Children between 15 and 17 can be detained in prison if the court agrees they are of unruly character.

Adopting a child

Adoption is a formal procedure which gives the adopting parents all the rights and duties of the child's natural parents who then lose those rights. The natural parents have to consent, no money must change hands and there must be a court order.

Adoptions can be arranged through local authorities, adoption societies or privately. You should contact your local council or CAB about it. You will normally have to go on a waiting list if you want to adopt a child and may have to wait a long time. Your application will be very carefully considered to make sure that you are 'suitable'. Generally married couples over 25 and under 40 with a good home and a reasonable income are the type of people preferred by adoption organizations.

The procedure for adoption

When you have been accepted for an adoption you have to look after the child for a trial period of at least three months. The adoption is formalized through the County Court or the juvenile court so they as well as the local authority must be informed. The agency or society arranging the adoption will tell you about this. A social worker or probation officer will report to the court about your suitability to have the child and they will also make enquiries of the child's natural parents as they have to consent. In rare cases the natural parents' consent can be dispensed with. There is a private hearing in the court and as long as the judge or magistrate is satisfied then the adoption order is made.

If you want your child adopted

You can arrange this by contacting the social services department of your local council or an adoption agency. Once an adoption order is made you lose all rights over your child. In most cases unless you have failed to look after your child you have to consent to the adoption and can withdraw your original consent at any time up to the making of the adoption order.

Fostering of children

Fostering is quite different from adoption. The foster parents never get full rights over the child. So foster parents have to agree to allow a foster child to be withdrawn by the local authority or the voluntary society which has placed the child. They are paid a fixed sum weekly, and look after the child for as long as required. The council will normally supervise the foster parents, and social workers will visit the child regularly. One of the aims of fostering is to keep the children in contact with their natural parents. Sometimes foster parents refuse to give up children to the natural parents. The only hope they have of keeping the child is to apply to make the child a ward of court and then ask for care and control of the child to be vested in them.

Illegitimate children and how to get maintenance

An unmarried woman who has a child is the only person with all the rights and duties of a parent. The father of the child has no rights at all. He can, however, be required to contribute to the child's maintenance. A mother can get maintenance by applying to a magistrates court for an affiliation order against the father. The application must be made within three years of the child's birth, but can be later if the father pays money for the child's upkeep before it is three years old. The mother goes to the court and asks for a summons which the police will serve on the father. If the alleged father disputes paternity, the mother will have to try and prove it by getting, for instance, a witness who has heard the man say he is the father of the child. The court has power to request blood tests if one of the parties asks for this, but neither party has to agree. If they refuse without good reason then this may go against them. Blood tests can show clearly that somebody is not the father but cannot prove that he is, only that he could be. Once the court decides to make an affiliation order they will award weekly maintenance in the same way as in matrimonial proceedings in the magistrates court (see page 62).

Your obligations about educating your child

Every child between 5 and 16 must receive full time education and it is the parents' duty to ensure they get it. Most children are educated in schools provided by the local education authority. You have no absolute right to choose a school, but your wishes about the type of school you want for your child should be met wherever possible. If you do not get your choice then you will have some chance of changing the mind of the local authority if you can show medical or religious reasons why you want your child to go to the school of your choice.

You must make sure that your child attends school, as if he does not, particularly if you have told him not to, you can be guilty of an offence. While at school, the teachers exercise parental powers and so can discipline children. They can also, depending on the policy of the education authority, use corporal punishment. Teachers cannot expel children from maintained schools but if the child does not, or will not, fit in he can be suspended and then transferred to another school. You can usually appeal to the governors or managers against this decision.

Family property

Problems about ownership of family property will only usually arise when the marriage has broken down. But after somebody dies there can often be disputes about how the dead person's property is distributed. The best way to avoid this is to make a will.

Making a will

A will is basically a written statement of your wishes as to where your property should go when you die. Anybody over 18 who understands what he or she is doing can make a valid will but there are various formalities that have to be followed.

Wills have to be in writing and dated, and then signed at the end by the testator who must be seen adding his signature by two witnesses. They must then add their signatures as witnesses while they are all still together.

It is sensible to make a will since it stops problems after your death. If your wishes are anything but very simple (e.g. everything to my wife) you should get a solicitor to draw up the will for you and legal aid is available for this. If you do not use a solicitor, then it is really very important that you use a will form, which you buy from a stationer. But the law interprets wills very strictly and many words used in wills do not have their ordinary meaning, so it is sensible to get legal advice.

You want to have at least two standard clauses in any will you make. One should revoke all previous wills you may have made, and the other should appoint an executor or executors. As they will have to see that the terms of the will are carried out, they should be asked first. A golden rule about will-making is to have totally independent witnesses since a witness cannot acquire any property left to him by the will.

Adding to a will. People often want to add things to their wills. You can do this by putting what is called a codicil at the end which has to be dated, signed and witnessed in the same way as a will. But codicils can create complications. So it is best to make a new will if you want to change or add any wishes. Once you have made a will, keep it in a safe place like a bank and tell somebody you trust where it is.

Distributing property after death

When the value of the property left by the deceased person is under £500 there is no need to go through the formalities of getting legal authority to deal with the estate. But if the value is over that then you have to go through the formal procedures.

The obligations of personal representatives

The estate has to be dealt with by personal representatives. They are appointed in the will if there is one and are called executors. Otherwise the closest next of kin are most usually appointed. They have to find the value of all the assets and debts and then get legal authority from the Probate Registry to distribute the estate. Various forms have to be completed and it is best to see a solicitor about this. Once probate is granted the personal representatives collect in the assets, pay estate duty and the debts and distribute the rest of the estate to those entitled.

Distribution where there is a will. The first job is to give the specific legacies to those entitled. Houses, land, shares and savings accounts have to be transferred into the name of the beneficiary so that they can be the full owner. There are often problems when the residuary estate, that is everything that is left after paying debts and distributing legacies, has to be divided between two or more people. It is best for everybody to agree on what each should have. If that cannot be done then it is sensible to sell things by auction and divide the money equally.

Distribution where there is no will. The husband or wife of the deceased person is absolutely entitled to the first £15 000 of the estate. If the property is worth more then the husband or wife gets half of everything above £15 000 after payment of estate duty. The children are entitled to the rest of the money in equal shares. If there is no husband or wife then the children are entitled to the estate in equal shares and if there are no children the money goes to other relatives, the parents first, brothers and sisters next and so on. You should get legal advice about this.

Challenging a will. Sometimes people make wills which leave their property away from their immediate family. A wife or husband can challenge this but you need to see a solicitor about it. The will can be varied by the court to look after the interests of wives, husbands and children.

6 Problems with Tax and Help from the State

Paying tax

Tax is paid on your income, including pensions, after various deductions have been made. The tax year runs from April to April. A married man who lives with or wholly maintains his wife gets a married man's personal allowance and an allowance for their children which varies with age. Mortgage interest payments, half of life insurance premiums and sometimes expenses from work can all be deducted. There are other allowances for the elderly, for widows or widowers with dependent children, for dependent relatives and housekeepers and for blind people. You should claim all you are entitled to when completing your tax form. You can go to your local Citizens Advice Bureau for help with completing tax forms. Solicitors will not normally provide this sort of service although accountants will, at a fee. Tax is paid by most people on what is left after deductions. There are two main ways of paying tax:

Tax for wage earners

Wage earners pay under the PAYE System. Each year most people have to complete a tax return (form P1) on which you give details of your income (including money from part time jobs), and on which you claim your allowances. If you are married and have a wife who is earning, her income should be included. A code is then issued by the Inspector of Taxes and your employers use this code to work out how much tax to deduct from your wages. You have a right of appeal against this decision (see page 80). Wives can be separately assessed but unless the wife earns a high salary there is no advantage in doing this. As long as you are continually employed throughout the tax year, the PAYE system normally results in your paying the right amount of tax. If you are unemployed for a time you may pay too much tax. It depends on how long you are out of work and when this happens in the tax year. Write to your tax inspector about overpayments. You can also have your code changed during the year if your circumstances change so that you become entitled to a higher allowance. So if for instance you marry or have a child or buy a house on mortgage this will increase your allowances and so reduce the amount of tax you have to pay. But you need to get your tax code changed by writing to the Tax Inspector.

Tax for self-employed people

The self-employed pay tax on their profits. Tax is assessed on earnings in the previous year and paid in two lump sums on 1 January and 1 July. So a small shopkeeper will pay tax in 1974 on the profit he made between April 1972 and April 1973. All self-employed people have to fill in a tax return (Form 11) and an assessment is then made against which you can appeal (see page 81).

Choosing to be self-employed or employed. The advantage of being self-employed is that you can claim many expenses as deductions against your income which PAYE payers cannot do. The disadvantage, and this creates a lot of problems, is that you are supposed to pay the tax in two lump sums and you may not have saved enough to do this. It is even more difficult to pay if your income has gone down. Self-employed people have to pay a higher insurance stamp as well and that can be difficult on a low income. Also if you do not keep accurate accounts of your earnings you may be assessed for tax on the basis that you have earned more than you in fact have. It is best to take advice about which system is best for you if you have a choice. You should see an accountant or a solicitor.

Tax avoidance and evasion

You are allowed to arrange your affairs so that you pay as little tax as is legally possible. So you should claim all your allowances to avoid paying too much tax. However, tax evasion, that is deliberately lying to or misleading the tax inspector so you pay too little tax, is unlawful. The whole tax system depends on people completing tax returns. You don't win by refusing to do this. Self-employed people will usually be assessed to pay a large lump sum in tax if they refuse to fill in the form. That forces you to appeal and you can then be made to give details of your income. PAYE payers may find they are not getting their full tax allowances because the inspector only has to give them if you claim them.

Appeals against tax assessments

You have a right of appeal against your tax assessment. If you are paying through PAYE and have paid too little or too much tax, or if you ask for one, you will get a notice of assessment. Self-employed people get this notice automatically. You have 30 days from receiving the notice in which to appeal.

* Firstly you write to the tax inspector saying you wish to appeal against the tax assessment and give your grounds. It is best to set them out in full but you can simply say the assessment is too high and give details later after taking advice.

* If you pay under PAYE and think the coding is wrong, give details as soon as possible, so the code can be changed. You may need an accountant's help when dealing with the inspector as you usually have to exchange a number of letters.

* The aim is to negotiate a settlement with the inspector which will avoid a tribunal hearing.

* But if you do not settle or decide not to drop the appeal then you can ask for the case to be heard by a tribunal. There are two tribunals, the Special Commissioners who deal with complicated legal points arising in tax cases and the General Commissioners who deal with everything else.

Appeals to the General Commissioners. General Commissioners are usually local people of some standing in the area and they hear cases in private. The procedure is informal. You or your representative if you have one, put your case and produce witnesses or documents if necessary. The tax inspector will always be there, and will question you and tell the tribunal in non-technical terms why he has reached his decision. You can then reply to his case. The Commissioners will usually ask questions of both sides. They then ask both you and the inspector to withdraw while they consider their decision in private. You have to prove to the Commissioners that the assessment is too high, and if you cannot, then the assessment will be confirmed. No costs can be awarded to either side.

Appeals to the Special Commissioners. Special Commissioners are tax lawyers, professional judges, who travel about the country hearing cases. It is best to have an accountant or solicitor to represent you since the arguments are usually very technical. The procedure is however the same as for the General Commissioners.

Further appeals from the Tax Commissioners. There is a further appeal to the High Court. If you want to take your case to the court you must tell the Commissioners you are dissatisfied when you get their decision and then within 30 days ask the clerk of the tribunal to state a case for a decision by the High Court. You will have to show the Commissioners have made a mistake about the law, as factual mistakes cannot, except in very exceptional circumstances, be challenged. Legal advice is essential if you want to appeal to the courts.

Help from the State

If people are unable to work or are not paid enough when working to feed and keep their families or pay their rent, then they may be eligible for financial help. There are three different types of schemes: those where income is given as of right, those where income is given subject to a means test and those where local councils provide benefits subject to a means or some other form of test.

Benefits paid as of right

Family Allowance. If you have two or more children you are entitled to a weekly family allowance of 90p for the second and £1·00 for each other child. The money is not meant solely for the benefit of the children but is for the benefit of the whole family. The allowance is usually paid to the mother by order book and is taxable. Problems arise when your children are not living with you or sometimes when the parents are not married. Usually the children have to be in your household but you may be able to claim if you support them unless they are in compulsory care of the local authority. Only the mother of illegitimate children can claim for them, not the father, and generally if at least one parent is alive nobody else can claim for the child. Disputes about entitlement can be dealt with by an appeal to a National Insurance Local Tribunal (see page 54). You should claim as soon as you think you are entitled on a form you can get from the Post Office.

Attendance allowances. People who are severely disabled and have been so for more than six months may be eligible for this benefit. It is paid to, or for, anybody over 2 years of age who needs attention in relation to their bodily functions or supervision to avoid danger to themselves or others. There is a higher rate for people who need help both by day and night, and a lower rate for those needing help at one or other of those times. There is no means test as the benefit is to compensate for the attendance given not for the financial loss you suffer as a result of having to look after somebody who is ill. Claim forms are obtained from the DHSS.

National Insurance Benefits. These benefits are paid subject to contributions you have made through paying weekly insurance stamps. Everybody over 16, unless they are exempt, has to pay. Married women, widows and people on very low incomes can be exempted from paying stamps. The most important benefits are for the unemployed, the sick, widows, people who suffer industrial injury or disablement and for those entitled to State retirement pensions. There are in addition maternity benefits, allowances for guardians, death grants and special allowances for children.

How to claim insurance benefits

Claims are made in different ways for each benefit, but if you are in doubt, then enquire at your local DHSS office. The contribution conditions differ for various benefits, but provided you satisfy them you will usually be eligible for the benefit itself, and for increases for dependants. So somebody who is sick may be eligible for benefit for himself, an increase for his wife if she is not earning more than the amount of the increase, and money for each of his children.

When benefits may be refused

Unemployment benefit can be stopped for six weeks if you are accused of having lost your job through misconduct or having left it without good cause and it will only last for twelve months in any event. Sickness benefit will be refused if you are thought to be capable of work. This benefit will stop after six months but if you are still ill you may be eligible for invalidity benefit. For the first five years after retirement you may lose your pension because you earn too much or carry on working full time. And widows can lose their benefits if they are accused of cohabiting with a man as his wife. Disputes often arise and benefit is denied because of late claims, so always claim quickly. If you are refused benefit you should appeal to the National Insurance Local Tribunal (see page 54).

Industrial Injury Benefit. If you have an injury at work or suffer from an industrial disease then you get a higher rate of benefit than for ordinary sickness. There are often disputes as to whether the injury actually happened at work. For instance, a man who felt dizzy after lifting a heavy weight, carried on working, and then went home and had a heart attack, might not be able to show that his heart attack was caused by the lifting, and so might be refused injury benefit. But you can appeal against such decisions to the Local Tribunal. Once you are able to work again you may be entitled to disablement benefit because of your loss of the ability to enjoy a normal life. This is assessed on a percentage basis and can be disputed before a medical appeal tribunal. On top of that, you might be eligible for special hardship allowance to make up your lost pay.

State means-tested benefits

The most important point to remember about the various benefits listed below is if you are in any doubt about whether you are entitled you should claim. You will not lose anything and you might gain!

Family Income Supplement for wage earners. Anybody on a low income, including a single person or unmarried couple, who is in full time work that is over 30 hours a week and has at least one dependent child may be eligible for this benefit. You claim on form FIS 1 obtainable from the local post office. The benefit is based on the difference between a set limit for your number of children and your average earnings over the previous five weeks. It lasts for twelve months and cannot be increased or decreased during that period even if your earnings go down or up. You can appeal to a Family Income Supplement Appeal Tribunal if you think you have been wrongly refused FIS (see page 54).

Supplementary benefits for people who are not working. Anybody who is not in full time work and whose income is less than the scale rates of supplementary benefit can claim. You get an allowance for yourself, for your children and for rent. Couples receive a higher rate. It is possible to increase your benefit for extra expenses like heating costs or for special diets for people who are ill. You can also claim extra lump sum grants to meet special expenses such as buying clothes and furniture if you need them. Benefit can be refused to women who are cohabiting with a man who has a job. There are also various control procedures which can reduce benefit below the scale rates, or force people to go out to work. These control procedures are not applied to pensioners. You should always appeal to the Supplementary Benefit Appeal Tribunal if you are refused benefit or extra grants. (For further details see *Supplementary Benefit Rights* by Ruth Lister.)

Rent and rate rebates for householders. Anybody who rents their home may be eligible for rent rebates. The rebate scheme covers council and housing association tenants, unfurnished tenants of private landlords and most furnished tenants. Your local council operates the scheme so get a claim form from the Town Hall. They calculate the amount of rebate by relating your income to a set scale for yourself and your dependants. Private tenants receive a regular giro. Council tenants simply pay the reduced rent. The rebate period ends after six months and you should then re-apply. You are supposed to tell the Council of any change in your financial circumstances during the rebate period.

Rate rebates can be given to anybody who pays rates on their own home. The calculations are done by the local council in a similar way to rent rebates. Get a claim form from the Town Hall.

Other benefits

There are many other benefits you may be eligible for. The most important are listed below and people who receive FIS or supplementary benefit are automatically eligible for most of them:

1. Free prescriptions for, among others, children, pensioners, expectant and nursing mothers, people with certain illnesses and people on low incomes.

2. Free welfare milk and foods for children and expectant or nursing mothers.

3. Free dental treatment, dentures and spectacles for children and young people and, among others, people on low incomes.

4. Free school meals for children of people on low incomes.

5. Educational benefits from the local authority including uniform grants, essential school clothing grants, travel to school, and maintenance grants for 16 to 18-year-olds.

6. Many local authorities have concessionary fares for old people and all have to provide assistance for chronically sick and disabled people and various services for the elderly.

You claim these benefits in various different ways. When in doubt ask at the local DHSS office, the Town Hall or a Citizens Advice Bureau.

7 Housing Problems

Renting a house from a private landlord

Probably the most difficult problem in renting houses is actually finding one to rent. They are advertised in local and national papers, in estate agents and accommodation agencies and on newsagents' bill boards. Prospective tenants are often asked to pay a fee for being given addresses, premiums for getting a home or money for fixtures and fittings.

Fees for addresses. It is a criminal offence for accommodation or estate agents to ask for or to accept money for putting your name on a list of prospective tenants or for simply giving the addresses of homes to let. Most agencies ignore the law and so if you badly need the house and have to pay the fee first then do so, and claim it back once you are in. Agents have a right to payment if they actually find you a house, but they must do a fair amount of work.

Premiums. Many landlords and some tenants assigning leases try to charge premiums or key money. This is illegal in most unfurnished lettings and in any furnished ones where the rent has been registered by a rent tribunal. If you do pay a premium you should get a receipt. Then take advice about claiming it back from a solicitor or a Citizens Advice Bureau. Your local council can also be asked to prosecute the landlord.

Fixtures and fittings. It is common for people to charge for fixtures and fittings. If the difference between the real value of the furniture and the price paid is considerable, this will be looked upon as a premium which you can recover. The sale of furniture and fittings at their proper value is not illegal.

Agreements and rent books. Once you have decided to take the property you may be asked to sign an agreement. Take some advice from a solicitor or a CAB before signing anything since there may be clauses particularly about repairs and assignments which may create problems.

Every tenant who pays rent weekly must have a rent book. It should have details in it about the landlord's name and address, that of his agent, the rent, the rates and details of the rebate schemes operating locally. Insist on getting a rent book, and complain to the council if the landlord refuses to provide one. Many landlords ask for a deposit. If you pay one you should get it back at the end of the tenancy.

Rent levels

Rents of property with a residential landlord. If your landlord lives on the premises and you are a furnished tenant or an unfurnished tenant who moved in after 12th August 1974, then you can have your rent fixed by a Rent Tribunal. The landlord cannot put the rent up at all unless he asks the Rent Tribunal to do this so it is worthwhile checking if the rent is registered. Whether or not the rent is registered you can apply to the Rent Tribunal to have it reduced. Get the tribunal's address from the Town Hall. The tribunal inspect the property, hold a hearing and fix the rent. They will also usually consider questions about security of tenure (see page 92). Should you discover you are paying more than the registered rent, you can claim the money back, and if necessary sue the landlord in the local County Court.

Rents of property with no residential landlord. Different rules apply depending on whether you are a protected or controlled tenant.

Protected tenancies. Landlords of property whether furnished, or unfurnished, which they do not also live in, cannot usually charge a higher rent on a new letting than they charged the last tenant during the past three years. This rule does not apply to increases in rates, and if there have been improvements or if the landlord has taken on further repairing responsibilities. If however the rent has been registered by the Rent Officer (check with him – the Town Hall will have his address) the landlord can only increase the rent within three years of the registration if the rates go up. They can get round this by asking you to sign a rent agreement but take advice before doing this. Rent agreements should be registered with the Rent Officer. Should you discover you are paying over a registered rent and you have not signed 'a new rent agreement you can recover rent overpaid for the last two years. Deduct it from your rent, or ask the landlord for it back. If necessary you sue in the County Court (see page 37).

Applying to have your rent registered. You can always apply to the rent officer to register a 'fair' rent. He takes into account the age, character, location and repair of the property and should ignore any question of scarcity. He inspects the property and has a consultation with you and the landlord at his office The Rent Officer can increase or decrease an unregistered rent, so it is sensible to find registered rents of properties similar to yours, before applying to have yours registered. The Rent Officer has a list of registered rents and will help you to find rents of similar properties to yours. If you find that your rent is already registered, it can only be reduced or more usually increased three years after the registration. There has to be some change of circumstances for that rule to be broken. Once the Rent Officer has reached a decision he registers the rent. Either side can appeal to a Rent Assessment Committee if they disagree with the rent fixed. You should take advice from a solicitor before appealing.

Controlled tenancies. These are tenancies where you will usually have been in occupation with a fixed rent since before 1957. If you have a controlled tenancy it used to be difficult for the landlord to increase your rent without improving your home. Now it is possible for the landlord to do this whether or not your home has basic amenities. These are a bath, handbasins, sink and hot water as well as a proper w.c. But you should make sure your rent is fixed by the Rent

Officer and not just enter into an agreement with your landlord. But if the landlord wants to do improvements rather
than simply have a rent fixed, you can still refuse to allow this.
It will force him to take you to the County Court if he really
wants to do some work. That has advantages, as the court
can fix the terms on which the improvements are to take
place. Any increase fixed by a Rent Officer of a formerly controlled rent has to be phased (consult your council). If you
decide not to go to the Rent Officer then you should be
sure to enter into a formal rent agreement with the landlord
as that has to provide for phasing of the increase as well.

Security for tenants of private landlords

Court orders and notices to quit

You cannot be forced to leave your property except by court
order. Proceedings have to be started by a notice to quit
which has to be in writing and expire on a rent day. The notice
has to give you at least four weeks. Do not leave because you
get a notice to quit and always take advice from a solicitor or
CAB on the validity of the notice and what to do about it.
Your rights to stay differ depending on whether or not you
are a tenant of a residential landlord and even if you are,
whether or not you are really a furnished tenant.

Are you furnished or unfurnished?

Many so-called furnished tenancies where there is a residential
landlord and where you have been in the property since before
12th August 1974 are really unfurnished. The residential
landlord has to prove you are furnished, so you can defend a
possession action by arguing you are unfurnished. A few sticks
of furniture does not make your home furnished. It depends
on how much rent can be assumed to be paid for the furniture,
as well as the value of the furniture to you. You need advice
from a solicitor and possibly a valuer to decide this.

Security where there is no residential landlord

These tenants are far more secure than most others. You
should not move if you get a notice to quit and the land-

lord has to take you to court if he wants to get you out. The court will only consider giving possession to the landlord in a limited number of circumstances, the more important of which are listed below:

1. The landlord can give you alternative accommodation which is suitable to you and your family's needs in relation to rent, size and nearness to work.

2. You are in arrears with the rent or have broken some other important term of your agreement.

3. You or somebody living with you has caused nuisance or annoyance to neighbours or have damaged the property or the furniture, or neglected them.

4. You have given notice to quit, the landlord has signed a contract to sell the house and you have not left.

5. Your landlord wants to move into your home himself and he can show he suffers greater hardship than you because of his need for the property. It is most important to remember that this rule can only be applied against you if your landlord lived in the property before December 1965.

6. The house went with a job which is now finished and your landlord needs it for another employee.

7. Your landlord has retired and wants to live in your home and told you before letting it that this might happen.

If the landlord can fit your case into one of these conditions the judge still must decide if it is reasonable to make a possession order. There are a few cases where the judge must make a possession order. They include cases where a former owner-occupier has let you the premises and told you he might want them back. He will get them back if he has lived elsewhere during your tenancy and wants the property for himself or a member of the family who lived with him when he was last there. Similarly, tenants of houses formerly used by people employed in agriculture will have to leave if the landlord wants to use the property once again for an agricultural employee.

Always take advice if the landlord wants to get you out and especially if he is offering you a sum of money to leave. It will probably be too little.

Security for tenants of residential landlords

These tenants do not have much security. If you have signed a lease for one specific period—e.g., 6 months – you cannot get that period extended by the Rent Tribunal. But you cannot be forced to leave until the period ends unless you have broken the lease in some way. When the 6 months is up, if the landlord refuses to renew the lease, you no longer have any right to remain there. But your landlord must still take you to court if you do not leave, although the judge will give him possession automatically. You will probably get 28 days in which to leave after the court hearing. Otherwise if you pay rent weekly or monthly you can be protected from eviction by Rent Tribunals. If you receive a notice to quit you should apply to the Rent Tribunal (address from the Town Hall) for an extension of your security within 28 days of receiving the notice. The tribunal will come and inspect the property and then hold a hearing. They can extend your security for up to six months and you can apply for further time before the end of that period. It is sensible to try and show you have been a good tenant and that other places are difficult to find. Eventually the tribunal will probably refuse to extend your security or you will decide not to apply again. If you do not leave the landlord must still take you to the County Court, but the judge will then give a possession order automatically.

Council and housing association tenants

Local councils have a duty to consider the housing needs in their district and to provide houses and flats if they think it necessary. You will normally have to be on a waiting list, often for many years, before you will get a council house. All councils operate some sort of points scheme and some publish them. The higher number of points you have, for instance for overcrowding, disrepair in your home, or for medical problems, the nearer you come to the top of the list. When you become eligible for a council house you should be offered a choice; do not automatically take the first home offered. You should complain to your local councillor if you feel you are not being fairly treated.

Housing associations are increasingly providing more housing. They usually have a waiting list and many of them take families from the council waiting list.

Security of tenure. Neither council nor most housing association tenants have any security of tenure. You have to rely on the council or the association not evicting you without very good reason. But you must look carefully at your rent book or agreement to see what you can and cannot do in your home, since if you break the terms you may get evicted.

Rent levels. Council rents are now supposed to be equivalent to 'fair rents' in the private sector and the rent levels are to be changed every three years. Increases should, however, be phased. You have no right of appeal against the level of your rent.

Housing association rents are fixed in much the same way as for private landlords. The association has to refer the tenancy to the Rent Officer for him to set the rent.

Unlawful eviction and harassment

If the landlord harasses you he is acting unlawfully and can be both sued for damages in the County Court and prosecuted in the magistrates court. You can also take out an injunction against him very quickly if he does any of these things, but you need legal advice. Harassment can be anything which interferes with the tenant's enjoyment of his home, including cutting off gas and electricity and removing doors, or making excessive noise with the intention of making you leave.

If the landlord evicts you without a court order he can again be prosecuted or sued for damages in the County Court. You can take out an injunction or even break your way back in again, but you should be careful about doing that. Call the police if you are being unlawfully evicted but they will normally only act to stop a breach of the peace.

Repairing difficulties

If you have problems of disrepair you must first find out whose responsibility it is to do the work. Look at your lease or rent book which may give some guide. But there are various obligations which the landlord cannot get out of:

Your landlord's obligations. In any tenancy of less than seven years, made after 24 October 1961, the landlord has an obligation to repair the structure and exterior of your home and keep the plumbing and gas fittings in proper working order. You must tell him of any defects or he will not be responsible for loss you suffer as a result. If the tenancy is controlled the landlord is responsible for all repairs excluding decoration if the rent is twice the gross rateable value in 1956 which it normally will be. Landlords of furnished properties must ensure the property is fit to live in at the start of the tenancy, as they must in certain houses let at very low rents.

Tenant's obligations. The repairing covenant is in your lease or rent book and it usually sets out your responsibility. Generally you will have to do decorations and make good small defects like broken door handles. If you have to 'keep in repair' according to your agreement then the property has to be kept up to the same sort of standard as it was when you took it. If you have to leave it in repair when you go, you may have to make it rather better than it was when you moved in.

Getting repairs done. Once you are satisfied the work should be done by your landlord, you must tell him. If he does nothing, you can do the work yourself and deduct the cost from your rent, but you should get advice from a solicitor before doing that. It is often useful to call in the Town Hall's Public Health Department. If they think the property is prejudicial to health or a nuisance they can require the landlord to carry out repairs. Common nuisances are dampness, blocked lavatories, leaking roofs, and broken sash cords. If your landlord fails to do the work the council can both do it themselves and take the landlord to court. You can take the landlord and that includes a local authority to court yourself using Section 99 of the Public Health Act if all else fails.

Sometimes the property is in such a bad state that the Public Health Department will require it to be closed and if that happens the council has a duty to re-house you. You can also try and get the council to take over the management of a multi-occupied house so that repairs are carried out by them.

Repairing obligations for council tenants. Council tenants are in much the same position as private tenants. The council is usually either responsible for or will do the repairs. If they refuse or are slow, complain to your councillor or you can take the council to the magistrates court if you can show the property is a public nuisance.

8 Job Problems

Contracts of employment

Obligation to give a contract

However you get your job there will always be a contract
whether verbally agreed at an interview or given in writing
when your job starts. Your employer is in fact bound within
13 weeks of your taking a job to give you written particulars
of the terms of your contract. This rule does not apply if you
work less than 21 hours a week. He may want you to sign a
contract in the form of a letter setting out the terms of your
job, so check it carefully before you sign. Despite the rules,
some employers do not give contracts of employment. If
you have not got a contract then you should talk to your
trade union representative or the local Department of
Employment Office.

What information does the employer have to give?

The written particulars you are given have to provide certain
specific information.

1. You must be told your pay scale or how pay is calculated
and when you are paid.

2. It should also show your working hours, holiday entitlement and holiday pay.

3. The statement must make it clear how much holiday pay
you are entitled to if your job ends when you have not taken
your holiday entitlement.

4. Information must also be given about sick pay, pension

schemes and the notice which either you or your employer must give to end the job.

5. You should also be told in writing how to set about dealing with any grievances you may have and of your right to join a trade union.

6. It is important to check that overtime rates are clearly stated and to look carefully at pension provisions and holiday pay and entitlements.

7. You might find yourself unable to take a holiday you have already booked unless you have that right to do so written in your contract.

Notice of leaving

You are entitled to certain minimum lengths of notice once you have worked for the firm for more than 13 weeks. You should get one week's notice for less than 2 years' service, 2 weeks for between 2 and 5 years, 4 weeks for between 5 and 10 years, 6 weeks for up to 15 years and 8 weeks for more than that. Your contract may entitle you to longer terms of notice than the minimum but it cannot reduce the minimum terms. If your contract does give notice periods you will have to abide by them as well.

Your position after taking the job

Once you take the job you have to obey any lawful orders from your employer, look after his interests and keep his trade secrets. You cannot be required to do work outside your contract, but you can of course agree to do this.

An employer has various obligations particularly in relation to your safety. If there is a change in your contract, a pay rise for instance, then your employer must let you know in writing or make sure you can easily read of the change by notice or in some other similar way. If any questions arise as to what the precise terms of the contract are and you cannot settle these by negotiation you can ask an Industrial Tribunal to decide what the terms should be.

Dismissal and redundancy

Leaving your job

You can of course leave your job at any time but only if the
employer has broken the contract can you technically leave
without giving notice. If you do go without notice, employers
sometimes hold on to wages they owe you. You can sue them
in the County Court but they might be able to claim damages
equivalent to a week or two's wages for your breach of contract. If you resign voluntarily or after a request from the
employer you might lose your right to unemployment benefit.
It is best in this case to arrange for your employer to give you
your full notice. As long as you are at work you are entitled
to your pay during notice periods. You may also be entitled
to holiday pay but unless this is clearly set out in a written
contract people usually have difficulty in getting it.

Sacking by your employer

If you are dismissed you should get the notice provided for
in your contract, or failing that the required minimum notice
which depends on how long you have worked. Employers can
however dispense with notice or even pay in lieu of notice if
they say you have been guilty of serious misconduct, refusing
to work, theft, persistent lateness and suchlike. You may well
have a claim if you are sacked. This can be either for damages,
compensation or redundancy.

Claiming damages for wrongful dismissal

Anybody who is dismissed without notice and not given pay
in lieu or anybody who leaves voluntarily because the employer has broken his contract may have a good claim for
damages. You have to sue in the County Court but it is often
not worth it as you rarely get a lot out of the action. If your
complaint is that you did not get your notice then that is the
maximum you will get. If you say you have been wrongly
dismissed then you may not be awarded much compensation.
That is because you have a duty to reduce the damage you

suffer by getting another job. It is unusual to be awarded more than the amount of money you might have earned if you had been given your full period of notice.

Claiming reinstatement or compensation

Anybody who is sacked for reasons other than redundancy, conduct or bad work may be entitled to claim reinstatement or compensation for unfair dismissal from an Industrial Tribunal. You have to have worked for your employer for at least 1 year. The only exception to this rule is if you are dismissed because of trade union activity. You have to complain within 6 months to an Industrial Tribunal, but time limit is important and vital, so consult your union immediately and put your claim in straight away.

The Industrial Tribunal hears both sides and has power to order your reinstatement or to give compensation. If either side refuses reinstatement then you can only get compensation. The compensation will be reduced if you unreasonably refuse reinstatement. Compensation can cover such things as loss of wages and pension rights as well as compensating you for the general loss of the job.

Claiming redundancy money

You may however be dismissed because there is no longer a job for you or your job is so changed that you should not reasonably be expected to do it. You are then technically redundant and entitled to redundancy pay. People who are on short time work for a long period may also be able to claim they are redundant.

To be entitled to redundancy pay you must have worked for more than 21 hours weekly for 2 years. Payment is based on your years of service, and your age. You get half a week's pay for each year you worked when aged 18 to 22, one week's pay for each year from 22 to 41 and one and a half weeks' pay for each year from 41 to retiring age (60 for women and 65 for men). But your redundancy money is scaled down when you near retirement age. The maximum service that can be taken

into account is 20 years' work and earnings over £80 a week
are disregarded. The redundancy money is calculated on your
normal weekly wage when you leave. It is vital to work any
notice you may be given as if you leave early because of
redundancy you might lose your entitlement to redundancy
pay. Normally you will be paid automatically but there are
of course disputes.

Disputes about redundancy pay. If you are not paid your redundancy money or if you dispute the amount then you can take
your case within 6 months to an Industrial Tribunal. Employers can avoid having to pay redundancy if they offer
suitable alternative employment but you might dispute that
it is suitable. Your refusal to take another job must be reasonable. A requirement to move 50 miles to the same job would
normally not be a suitable alternative but a similar job in
the same area might be. If the firm has gone bankrupt and
you are then made redundant you will still be able to get
redundancy although this may be paid by the Department of
Employment. If you have to go to the Industrial Tribunal it
is advisable to be represented by your trade union or a
lawyer if you can arrange this.

Safety, accidents and injury at work

Safety at work

Employers must provide a safe system of work. This means
the work place, the tools and the machines you use have to
be safe and the employer has to make sure the staff is com-
petent. The Factory Acts set out safety regulations and they
have to be displayed at work. If you think the rules are being
broken then complain to your employer or get the trade
union to, and if nothing is done then complain to the Factory
Inspectorate. You can get their address from the local
Department of Employment Office. Employers can be fined
and imprisoned for breaking the rules and it is possible for
employees to be fined as well. You are entitled to a reasonable
temperature at work, adequate washing and toilet facilities,

enough light, fenced machinery and so on. Some industries like mines and shipping have particularly tough safety laws.

Claims for injury at work

If you are injured at work you may have two different types of claim. You can get injury and disablement benefit from the National Insurance Fund and you might be able to sue your employer for damages.

All accidents, however trivial, should be reported and if there is an accident book, as there must be in nearly all factories, then have the accident recorded. If you cannot do that write a letter to your employer and keep a copy. These precautions might help a claim later as, although you may not be immediately badly hurt, there could be complications. It is wise, even if you are not off work and certainly if you are, to get a certificate from your doctor showing what your injury was. It is always very useful to collect evidence from workmates and from witnesses to the accident and even to take photographs if you can. This preliminary work can save much time if disputes arise.

Claiming injury benefit from the State. You claim injury benefit by filling in the back of the National Health medical certificate which your doctor gives you and sending it to the Department of Health and Social Security. If you are self-employed then you can only get sickness benefit. Injury benefit is paid if the accident was in the course of your employment so you may be disqualified if you hurt yourself while fooling about, but claim anyway. You get increases for dependants and earnings related supplement. Injury benefit is paid for 26 weeks and then if you are still off work you may be eligible for sickness or invalidity benefit.

Disablement benefit for loss of faculty. In addition if you have suffered a temporary or permanent loss of your ability to enjoy life as others of your age do, you may be eligible for disablement benefit after 6 months. You should enquire at your local social security office. Disablement benefit is

assessed on a percentage basis related to your 'loss of faculty'.
If you are awarded over 20 per cent you get a pension. If the
percentage is less you will be awarded a lump sum. There are
other benefits like special hardship allowance which compensate you additionally for your inability to continue in work
or to earn as much as you used to do. Disablement benefits
are paid irrespective of whether you are eventually able to go
back to work.

People who suffer from industrial diseases

The system set out above operates if instead of being injured
you suffer from an industrial disease. Some types of work or
process can give you 'prescribed diseases'. You have to show
you worked with a particular material and that you have
contracted a prescribed disease associated with the material.
You may then get injury and disablement benefit. The most
famous example is pneumoconiosis, a lung disease, which
coal miners contract from breathing in coal dust.

*Benefits for families of people who die from industrial injury or
disease.* There are similar benefits paid by the State if somebody dies as a result of an industrial accident or disease.
Industrial widows pensions may be increased by an allowance
for children and parents and other relatives can sometimes
get a pension or a lump sum if the deceased maintained them.
You claim on the back of the death certificate and send it to
the DHSS.

Appeals against refusals of benefit

There is of course an appeal system if you are denied injury
or disablement benefit or if you think you have not been
awarded enough. Injury is dealt with by National Insurance
Local Tribunals, and disablement by Medical Boards and
Medical Appeal Tribunals (see page 54).

Suing your employer for damages

As well as claiming State benefits you may be able to sue your
employer for damages for the injury or disease you suffer from.

He has a duty to provide a safe system of work and if you can show he broke that duty and you have suffered an accident as a result then you have a claim. You should consult your trade union in all cases or a solicitor or the local Citizens Advice Bureau. Employers must all have insurance nowadays so if you win it will be the insurance company who pays the damages.

9 Consumer Problems

Faulty goods

Buying faulty goods

It used to be easy for sellers to exclude liability for faulty goods. One trick was to give guarantees which, although they meant you could get repairs done, excluded your rights to reject the goods. Now 'exemption clauses' in consumer sales are unlawful except in a few cases. This means that when you buy something, the seller in effect guarantees that the goods are of 'merchantable quality'. That means the goods must be fit for the purpose for which they have been bought, although a very low price might sometimes exclude this rule. The rule only applies to business sales, so in a private sale between ordinary people you can still exclude liability for faulty goods.

Faults which you cannot complain about

If there is a fault which is brought to your attention when you buy the object then you cannot complain about that. Similarly if you examine the goods before actually buying them and the examination ought to have revealed the defect, then you will not be able to complain. So, if you buy a car which you look at casually and it turns out to have a faulty clutch, you would probably be able to get reimbursement. But not if you buy a car which has scratches on it. If you buy goods at an auction, you cannot usually complain unless the thing you buy is not like its description in the catalogue.

Faulty goods bought on HP

In HP agreements the goods are still owned by the finance company, so they will have to replace or repair faulty goods free of charge unless they have set out the defects in the agreement. They cannot get out of this by exemption clauses.

Claiming compensation for faulty goods

If there is something wrong with your purchase you can always take it back and ask for your money to be returned. But there are many situations where you will not want to do that. You can ask the seller to repair the goods or replace them with a similar article. The shop might offer to give you part of the purchase price back or offer you something else. It is also common to give credit notes. You can demand cash instead of the note.

Should you be unable to work out a satisfactory compromise with the seller then as a last resort you can sue him either in the Small Claims Court, if the value is less than £75, or in the County Court proper (see page 38). It is best to get legal advice before doing this but you should do it soon after you discover the fault.

If you make a claim against the retailer you can get damages to cover any expenses you incurred because of the defect as well as the return of the purchase price. If you suffer some damage because of a fault in the goods which arose due to negligence by the manufacturers then you can claim against them rather than the retailer, but you have to show you have suffered some damage. So if a faulty cooker explodes and injures you the manufacturer may be liable. You might also have a claim against the retailer if you can show he ought to have known of the fault.

Buying goods on credit

There are many ways of buying on credit. You can use credit cards, bank loans and budget accounts or go to a finance house or a money-lender. Rates of interest are often very high and the borrowing is simply a cash transaction which provides the money to spend on goods. But the most popular method of purchasing goods on credit is hire purchase, where you buy by instalments. The outstanding instalment purchase debt is over two thousand million pounds and the hire purchase business continues to expand.

Different types of HP agreement

Most people call instalment buying HP. But there are two different types of agreements commonly used by sellers, hire purchase and credit sale. A third type, a conditional sale agreement, is virtually the same as hire purchase.

A hire purchase agreement is not really a sale at all but simply gives the buyer the right to buy the goods in due course.

In a credit sale agreement the buyer becomes the owner of the goods immediately although the price is paid by instalments.

Hire purchase was developed to help people obtain purchases quickly without paying the full price. Equally importantly it was designed to ensure that the seller could snatch the goods back if necessary, as until the full price is paid they remain the seller's property. So buyers have had to be protected against over-anxious sellers.

Standard clauses in HP agreements

All HP agreements, whatever they are technically, have various points in common. You must normally put down a deposit and then you take possession of the goods and pay the rest of the money by instalments over a fixed period. You are charged interest on the purchase price so you pay more than if you had bought outright. And if you do not keep up the payments you can be taken to court or be made to return the goods.

How HP agreements are made

The money to buy the goods is usually provided by a finance company which will work in closely with the shop or person you buy the goods from. So if you buy a car on HP you pay a deposit to the garage. You complete hire purchase forms and the garage sells the car to a finance company which then 'hires' the car to you. The garage keeps the deposit and is paid the rest of the price by the finance company. You pay the instalments to the company or sometimes to the garage if the garage acts as a collecting agent and when all the money is paid the car is yours.

Deposits and interest rates

The minimum deposit is fixed in many cases by the Government so it is impossible to get round it. But the interest rate is normally based on the whole purchase price. Interest of 10 per cent on £600 over 2 years usually means that throughout the 2 years you are paying 10 per cent on the whole of the money. At the end of the period when there is little of the £600 left to pay you are still paying 10 per cent interest on £600. The true rate of interest should be stated in all credit agreements.

Cancelling an HP agreement

If you sign the agreement on trade premises then you cannot cancel. But if the agreement is signed at home then you have to be sent a copy within 7 days. You can then cancel within 3 days. The goods will have to be returned to the seller or you can refuse to accept delivery if they arrive later. The seller must send back your deposit in full. If you cannot get the deposit back you will have to sue for it in the County Court. This right of cancellation does not apply if the HP price (the cash price of the goods plus the interest) was more than £2000.

Non-payment of instalments

If you cannot pay the instalments on a hire purchase or conditional sale agreement then as long as they cost less than £2000 you can send them back. But usually you will have to make up half the total purchase price and pay all the instalments unpaid up to the time you return the goods. If you find you cannot pay it's usually better to wait to let the hire purchase company make the first move. They can snatch back the goods if you have paid less than one third of the purchase price. Otherwise they have to sue you for the return of the

goods. They might try to persuade you to hand the goods
back but if you do then the 'half of the price rule' will operate
against you. Once they take you to court the judge can allow
you to retain the goods and may reduce the payments and
spread them over a longer period. Get advice from a CAB
or a solicitor if you are running into difficulties. If the HP
price of the goods and interest was more than £2000 then the
finance company can take them back without a court order.

If you have bought on a credit sale agreement then you have
no right to send the goods back if you can't pay the instalments. Should you fail to pay then the finance company
can sue to recover the whole debt and the court may order the
goods to be seized.

Selling the goods

If you have bought on hire purchase proper then you cannot
sell without the agreement of the finance company. They will
want all their money before they agree to allow you to do this.
Anybody who has bought on credit sale can sell at any time
but will in most cases be required to repay the whole price
straightaway.

10 Police Powers and Problems after Arrest

Police Powers

The police are an essential element in the legal system. They provide protection for the citizen. In order to fulfil their role they have some special powers which it is useful to know about, but, equally, the citizen has his or her rights too.

Police powers in the street

If a policeman stops you in the street and questions you then it is usually sensible to answer him. But except in a few cases there is no obligation for you to reply. There are exceptions and the most important is motoring cases. A driver who is asked his name and address by the police must give it. If he refuses he can be arrested and charged with obstructing the policeman in the execution of his duty. Equally if a policeman asks you to go with him to the police station you have no duty to do so. He must arrest you first and the police are reluctant to do this unless they are satisfied they can really proceed against you. Wrongful arrests can lead to a claim in the civil courts for damages.

Helping the police with their enquiries

It is very common for people to be questioned at a police station without being arrested. They are said to be helping the police with their enquiries. If you agree to do this it is wise to try and get a solicitor to come with you and to ask him to do this before you go. Once you are in the station you have a right to ask to phone your solicitor. But the police can still refuse to let your solicitor see you, and they often do, particularly if they think his presence would hinder the 'administration of justice'.

The right of silence. If you are helping the police with their enquiries or have agreed to be asked questions your most important right is to remain silent. It is often said that people who refuse to answer questions stand a better chance of avoiding conviction than anyone else. But obviously if you are convinced of your innocence it may be quicker and easier to answer police questions to clear the matter up.

The limits on police questioning. Obviously a policeman's aim when questioning somebody he thinks has committed an offence is to get evidence which can be used against him in a prosecution. They can ask any questions they like but they must not subject you to undue pressure. This is because any statement that you make has to be voluntary to be approved of by the courts as reliable evidence. The police will want a statement from you but if they offer you some inducement or frighten you into making the statement it may be held by a court to be inadmissible. So they should not say things like 'we can make it easier for you if you confess'. Nor should they threaten you to make you give a statement. But the police do often obtain statements by suggesting they will only prosecute for a minor as opposed to a major offence. And at the extreme they sometimes agree not to prosecute at all if you turn Queen's evidence against the other people suspected of the crime.

There are in fact a set of rules, known as the Judge's Rules, which limit the way in which a policeman can question you.

The rules require them to caution you once they suspect you of having committed an offence.

They have to tell you that you are not obliged to say anything but anything you say may be put in writing and used in evidence. That warns you of your right to remain silent. The caution often comes late in the questioning and defence lawyers often complain that the caution should have been given at an earlier time than in fact it was. But the Judge's Rules are not legally binding and the trial court can always ignore any breach of them.

Police searches in the street

The police have no general right to search people in the street. But there are some specific offences where they can do this. They can search you or your vehicle if they have reason to suspect that you are carrying dangerous drugs. Some police forces, particularly the Metropolitan Police, have power to search you on reasonable suspicion that you are carrying stolen goods. 'Reasonable suspicion' is difficult to define. If the suspicion was unreasonable then you could sue for damages but it is very difficult to win a case like this. In any event the police can usually say that they had information that, for instance, a thief was at work in the area where you were searched. The only remedy if you are angry about police behaviour is often a complaint to the Chief Constable. Most people will however usually agree to be searched.

Police searches in your home

Unless you give permission for a search of your home the police will generally need a warrant. The same rule applies to business premises. They obtain warrants from a magistrate by answering on oath that they have some ground for believing that there are, for instance, stolen goods on the premises. It is common practice for the police to search people's homes after they have been arrested. The law is unclear as to whether this is allowed but it is done none the less.

The right to enter your home without a search warrant does exist in a few cases. They can enter to arrest somebody who they believe has committed an 'arrestable offence'. That is an offence which carries a maximum penalty of more than 5 years' imprisonment. They can come into your home to prevent a breach of the peace or if there is a danger to life because of explosives. In addition if you have been convicted of handling stolen goods or some other dishonesty within the previous 5 years, the police do not need a warrant to enter and search. Obviously if there is an emergency the police or even private individuals can enter and search your home as long as there is some danger to life or the chance of severe damage to property.

Identification parades

Many convictions turn on identification. You are not obliged to join an identification parade though you have a right to ask for one if you wish. It is always wise to have a solicitor with you so do not agree to go on a parade without taking legal advice. You should for instance object to a parade which has people in it who do not look alike. If you have been picked out on an identification parade try and find out if the witness saw a photograph of you beforehand. Your lawyer might be able to object to the evidence being brought up in court if that has happened.

Photographs and fingerprints

The police have no automatic right to take photographs and fingerprints. In particular they need a magistrates court order to force you to give your fingerprints if you refuse to do so. They should destroy the prints and the photographs if you are acquitted or not proceeded against but that does not always happen.

Helping the police

You will be faced with difficult choices if the police think you have committed an offence. Standing on your rights, like the right to silence and the right not to have your fingerprints taken, may create considerable difficulties. The police might, for instance, refuse to let you out on bail when normally they would allow this or try and have you remanded in custody by the magistrates.

The rule that you have no duty to help the police is limited by the right of a policeman in an emergency situation to appeal for help. You have to assist him then. Should you decide to help the police or 'have a go' then you can use reasonable force to stop a crime or to arrest somebody. It is wise to be careful if you think of 'having a go' as you might be injured. You must not however help somebody avoid arrest if you are intending to hinder the police. That itself is an offence.

Complaints against the police

If you have been wrongly arrested or searched or if you have been injured by a policeman exceeding his powers then you can sue for damages in the civil courts. But take legal advice first as it is usually difficult to prove your case. You can however also complain about police behaviour. They are public servants and must therefore act scrupulously within their powers and avoid rudeness. You should complain in writing to the Chief Constable although you can go into the police station and make a verbal complaint. Investigation is carried out in private by another police officer and you will only ever be told the decision not the reasons why it was reached. The most you can usually hope for is an apology, although complaints can have a bad effect on a policeman's career. You should also be sure of your grounds before making a complaint since if it is made maliciously the officer can sue for libel or slander.

Problems after Arrest

There are hundreds of crimes which can be committed and millions are in fact committed annually. It is impossible to summarize them here but there are various things you should do if you run into trouble.

What to do after arrest

Applying for bail. You can ask to telephone a solicitor or friend when being held in the police station but this right is often refused. Anyway, few solicitors are willing to come at any hour to see you in the station. So you usually need to be free to get legal help.

You should ask the police to give you bail. If they have arrested you on a warrant issued by a magistrate it may have instructions at the back about granting you bail. If it does not, or if you have been arrested without a warrant, then the police decide whether or not to grant bail.

The grounds on which the police will grant bail. The decision has to be taken by a senior officer. He will consider how serious the offence is so he will be unlikely to give you bail if you are charged with robbery but might if the charge was simple assault.

Secondly, he will take into account the likelihood of your appearing in court. So somebody who has defaulted on bail before or who has no fixed address will be unlikely to get bail. Finally he must consider your personal circumstances. If you have a steady job, fixed address and a family to look after you, you have a good chance of bail if the charge is not serious.

Whatever happens, if there is no chance of you being brought to court within 24 hours of arrest the police must consider bail and should be reminded of this. The problem most often arises with arrests on Saturday.

Giving a recognizance for bail. You will always be asked to give a guarantee or recognizance that you will turn up at the court. The amount of money is fixed by the police but you do not have to produce it. Should you fail to attend court at the right time the court can order you to pay the money over whether you are found guilty or innocent.

Sureties. It is very common in the more serious sort of case or where the police think the accused has little money, to ask for sureties. They can require any number of sureties but it is unusual to ask for more than two. A surety guarantees that the accused will attend court at the time required. He stands surety for a sum of money set by the police but he does not have to produce the money. If, however, the accused person fails to attend court the surety can be ordered to pay the guaranteed sum and cannot claim it back from the person who should have stood trial. So the police will need to be satisfied you could pay the money if necessary. That is why they prefer householders or people earning good wages.

Bail from the court. If the police refuse bail then you must ask for it when you appear before the court. Once you are there the decision about future bail rests entirely with the magistrates. But the police will always tell the magistrates whether or not they object to bail. If they do not object then the magistrates usually grant it. But when they do object they will normally give their reasons and you or your lawyer will have to argue against them.

Grounds for getting bail from the court. You stand the best chance of getting bail if you give as much information as possible, so you should tell the magistrates about your home and family circumstances. Where you live and how long you have been there. Whether you rent or own your home. What your job is and how long you have had it. Whether you have had bail before without any problems arising.

If they decide to grant bail the magistrates will also fix a money recognizance which you do not have to pay unless you default. They may also ask for sureties. You or your lawyer can argue against the sums fixed or asked for by the police, but it is difficult to get them reduced. The sureties will be for a fixed sum and it is usual for the police to accept or reject the people who come forward. You can ask the magistrates to see the proposed surety if the police object to him or her.

Obviously it is sensible to talk to the police officer in charge of your case before coming into court to ask him what his attitude will be to a request for bail. Ask him about sureties as well and if he wants these try and telephone people who can arrange to be sureties.

Sometimes it is impossible to get bail in the first court appearance. The police may object, the sureties may be unavailable, the court may not grant it. You will then be remanded in custody, usually for a week, and you can apply again the next time you appear. The week will give you and friends a chance to organize sureties, talk to the police and get a lawyer to make the bail application.

The dangers of being a surety. The police check out everybody who offers himself as a surety, but once accepted then the surety has various responsibilities. He signs a form agreeing to pay the sum fixed if the accused fails to attend court. So it is wise to keep in contact with the person you are standing surety for to see he does not run off. Sureties can in fact arrest the people they are standing bail for. But it is better to go to the police if you think your bail may disappear and ask them to arrest him or to be released from your surety. If they refuse, you can go and ask the magistrate to do this.

Once the accused turns up at court for trial the surety's responsibilities end. But the courts are tough on sureties when the accused does not appear. They will normally order them to pay the money they have guaranteed.

Appeals against a refusal of bail. If the magistrates refuse bail you can appeal to the judge in chambers. You must be told of this right by the clerk of the court and can ask for reasons. It is best to have a solicitor to organize the appeal for you but he cannot get legal aid for this so you may be in difficulties. If not you should write to the Official Solicitor from the prison where you are being held. Ask the prison officers for a special letter and outline in full why you need bail and your family responsibilities in the same way as on page 115.

Getting a lawyer for your case

If you are arrested and held in a police station you must ask to telephone a solicitor if you have one or a friend (see above). Try to get them to come and see you in the police station but whatever happens you will want somebody, preferably a lawyer, in the court when you appear. A friend can try and get hold of a solicitor to appear for you but many will be reluctant to do this unless you have legal aid.

In some areas there are duty solicitor schemes operating so ask the gaoler about this. A solicitor will be in the court building and will see anybody who asks for help and he or she normally gives advice under the green form scheme (see page 28). The solicitor will advise you and may apply for bail, an adjournment or legal aid on your behalf. If the case is simple he may represent you in the court on that day and if you want to plead guilty he should be asked to make a plea in mitigation for you. That means he should do his best to tell the court why the penalty should not be particularly severe.

If there is no duty solicitor and you do not intend to plead guilty or you want legal help then ask for legal aid. The magistrates will grant or refuse it or may ask you to fill in an application form.

You can choose a solicitor from a list which the court officials have. It is best to get a friend's recommendation but if all else fails ask the officials for advice.

Applying for an adjournment of your case

When you first come to court after an arrest it is quite likely that the police will not be ready to argue the case. They will then ask for an adjournment, technically called a remand, which is usually granted. You should ask for bail and legal aid. If the police want to go ahead and you do not, then ask for an adjournment, bail and legal aid yourself. You should tell the magistrates why you want an adjournment. You will, for instance, probably want legal advice, or may need to contact witnesses. Adjournments are usually for a week but may be longer if you are on bail and the case is going to take some time to argue.

Some other Arrow titles which might be of interest

CITIZENS RIGHTS SERIES
General Editor: Frank Field
Director of the Child Poverty Action Group

The legislation of the Welfare State aimed to give ordinary people a much better deal. But politicians and lawyers overlooked one crucial fact. We don't all speak or understand their language.

Unlike the official handouts this series is written by experts whose work is to help people understand and claim their rights. In other words it has been written with you in mind.

Each guide can be read without referring to any other material. They can deal with all the main issues where you, the citizen, find that 'they' are not telling you all you ought to know.

Supplementary Benefit Rights

by Ruth Lister   50p

Supplementary Benefit Rights will tell you
★ how to claim your supplementary benefit
★ how much benefit you should be getting
★ how to get more than the basic rate
★ what to do if your benefit is reduced, refused or stopped
★ how to appeal if you're not satisfied

Other books in this series are in preparation.

An Arrow Special

Unequal Britain
A Report on the Cycle of Inequality

by Frank Field   50p

Has the Welfare State made British society more equal since the war?

Frank Field, Director of the Child Poverty Action Group, draws together evidence from all the major social reports to ask if there is a cycle of inequality in which a large number of people are trapped. The report examines

★ Whether all British children have an equal chance of surviving birth?
★ Does the education system make society more or less equal?
★ Have income differentials between rich and poor changed since the war?
★ Are income inequalities reflected in the work place?
★ Do the rich enjoy better health?
★ Do the poor have equal access to a decent home?
★ Is wealth becoming more evenly distributed?

An Arrow Special

Born to Fail?

by Peter Wedge and Hilary Prosser   35p

The National Children's Bureau reports on striking
differences in the lives of British children

Of all the children born in Britain in the week of
3–9 March 1958

★ 1 in 4 have grown up in a family with 5 or more
  children or with only one parent
★ 1 in 4 have been living in bad housing
★ 1 in 7 have been in low income families

Any one of these experiences may be hard enough for a
child to overcome

But 1 in 16 children – on average 2 in every British
classroom – have to face all three situations

Born to Fail? shows the massive accumulation of additional
hardships that confront this group of children in almost
every aspect of their daily lives.

What do we expect to become of them?
What should we do to help them?

Breaking Up
A Practical Guide to Separation, Divorce and Coping on Your Own

by Rosemary Simon   65p

No divorce is entirely free of worry and hardship. Difficult questions concerning children, money and the family home have to be resolved—as well as the daunting problems of coping on your own and the painful business of picking up the pieces and starting life afresh.

★ How do you get a separation or divorce?
★ What are your rights to the family home?
★ Do you qualify for legal aid?
★ What should you know about maintenance?
★ Who can assist if you are short of money?
★ How can you find accommodation?
★ What about your children?
★ Where can you meet new friends?
★ What are the challenges of a second marriage?
★ Whom can you turn to for help with problems?

This book provides the answers to these and many other critical questions.

The Union Makes Us Strong

The British Working Class Its Politics and Trade Unionism

by Tony Lane   70p

Central to an understanding of the political condition of the working class is its one durable monument: the trades unions. Traditionally the working man has looked to his union – and its political arm, the Labour Party – for the power to bring radical change. But this book argues that the origins and structure of these organisations can only act for the accommodation of labour with capital.

By considering the history of the labour movement Tony Lane looks at the political consciousness of the rank and file, and the ways in which union leaders at all levels tend to become isolated from the man on the shop floor. In particular he explodes the cherished myth that the failures of socialism can be laid at the doors of a succession of leaders who have 'betrayed' the movement. His conclusion is that the power to force much needed social change must be spear-headed by a socialist party.

Tony Lane is lecturer in sociology at Liverpool University and Trevor Skempton who drew the illustrations is an architect.

Scrounging on the Welfare
The Scandal of the Four Week Rule

by Molly Meacher   60p

What is the four week rule?
Single unskilled men under 45 have had their Supplementary
Benefit stopped after only four weeks if the Employment
Exchange have indicated that unskilled jobs are available
in the area.

Why was it introduced?
To prevent the unemployed from leading a comfortable life
at the taxpayer's expense.

Has it worked?
Molly Meacher shows how little of the taxpayer's money
the rule has saved; how much unnecessary hardship it has
inflicted; how difficult it has been to operate the rule fairly.

Have the consequences of the rule amounted to a scandal?
Molly Meacher argues convincingly that they have. If the
Welfare system is to live up to its name, then fundamental
reforms will be necessary.

An Arrow Action Special

Out of Mind

by David Ennals   50p

The facts about mental health

> in 1961 there were 172,000 psychiatric new out-patients
> by 1970 this figure had increased to 227,000

> in 1964 370,000 people attended psychiatric day hospitals
> in 1970 there were over 1 million

> in 1970/71 38 million working days were lost through
> mental illness—many more than through strikes

> within the next 10 years more than 1 million of us will
> seek psychiatric help

Mental illness is now the biggest health problem of all. But
it is still the poor relation in the Health Service.

David Ennals, former Director of the MIND campaign,
looks at the issues and proposes a plan for urgent action.

It is time that we all faced the consequences of a disease on
the increase and helped the casualties of the way we live.

Education or Domination?
A Critical Look at Educational Problems Today

Edited by Douglas Holly   £1.00

This collection of original essays looks at critical alternatives to the theory and practice of education today.

Education and Politics
by *Ted Benton*

Economists and 'Human Capital'
by *Adam Westoby*

The Invisible Ruling Class
by *Douglas Holly*

Language and Class
by *Harold Rosen*

The Politics of Culture
by *Graham Murdock*

Integrating Art into Society
by *Ian Jeffrey*

Education, Race and Society
by *Charles Husband*

The School and The Community
by *Ken Worpole*

Relationships Among Teachers
by *Arnold Downes*

The Free Schoolers
by *Guy Neave*

Meet Your Friendly Social System

by Peter Laurie   £1.25

In moments of despondency we say, 'Well that's the system.
You can't beat the system'. But what is the 'system'? How
does it work? And how does it manipulate us?

Peter Laurie's new book looks at the ways the system
controls us. His examination reveals not a conspiracy of
cunning men but an inescapable social structure in which
each of us is locked rigidly into his place. He argues that
nearly every feature of our lives – poverty, good taste,
shiny shoes, sex, social workers, crime, dope, pension
funds – contributes to this iron pattern; and that before
we can change it, we must understand it.

This is a very unsettling book, but one that will strike a
chord in anyone who suspects that the world has gone awry.
Before the world can get better it will have to get worse.
But how much worse? Certainly after reading this book it
will never look the same again.

An Arrow Special

Low Pay

Edited by Frank Field   50p

Who are the low paid? Is low pay reinforced by other
inequalities? Why do some industries have a tradition of
low pay? How can we tackle low pay?

The contributors to this book examine the whole spectrum
of low pay and propose solutions to this increasingly
critical social problem.

Nicholas Bosanquet
The Real Low Pay Problem

Frank Field and Stephen Winyard
Low Pay in Public Employment and Wages Councils

David Stephen
Immigrant Workers and Low Pay

David Layton
Low Pay and Collective Bargaining

A. B. Atkinson
Low Pay and the Cycle of Poverty

Roy Moore
Low Pay and Fiscal Policy

Frank Field
Low Pay and Social Policy